café life ROME

A Guidebook to the Cafés and Bars
of the Eternal City

Written by Joe Wolff
Photography by Roger Paperno

ARRIS BOOKS
An imprint of Arris Publishing Ltd
Gloucestershire

First published in 2003 by

Arris Books
An imprint of Arris Publishing Ltd
Unit 1A Fosseway Business Centre
Stratford Road
Moreton-in-Marsh
Gloucestershire GL56 9NQ
www.arrisbooks.com

Text copyright © Joe Wolff 2003
Photography copyright © Roger Paperno 2003
Design copyright © Interlink Publishing 2003

ISBN 1 84437 008 9

Printed and bound in Korea

Book design by Juliana Spear

To request our complete catalog, please call us
at **01608 652655**, visit our web site at:
www.arrisbooks.com, or e-mail us at:
info@arrisbooks.com

CONTENTS

INTRODUCTION

*R*ome is a city full of cafés or bars (the terms are interchangeable)—about 8,000 in total. That's a lot of bars. So what we've done is go to the *centro storico* (downtown) and choose 22 Roman bars that we like, and we think you'll want to visit on your next trip to the eternal city. There are both the famous and the yet to be discovered. Most are family-run, passed down from one generation to the next; some are a hundred years old in buildings that are hundreds of years old. Each has a story to tell, a family history that we got straight from the horse's mouth by interviewing the proprietor.

We've collected this information for you in *Café Life Rome*, along with photos of the owners, the cafés, and the neighborhood. All of the cafés are within walking distance of each other. There's one thing to remember when you're wandering around the winding streets of the *centro storico*, a little disoriented, and you ask an Italian for directions (which soon becomes a group of two or three or more in a spirited discussion). You may hear the phrase, "*quella stradina li*" (that little street over there) accompanied by some pointing. This phrase is the kiss of death. It means no one has a clue, and they're just being polite. This phrase is your cue to bow out gracefully, consult your map, again, or whatever… that is if you ever want to arrive at your destination.

Armed with our informative little guide, you'll be one up on the other visitors and probably even some of the locals. The establishments we've profiled offer economical food and drink; maybe a pastry that is a specialty of the house or a type of *panino* (sandwich) or *focaccia* made only there. And of course, excellent espresso (they call it "*caffè*"). It's hard to find bad coffee in Rome, and we've chosen places that have the best. And since this is Italy, the land of gelato, we've also thrown five bar/gelaterias into the mix. Again, these are family-run establishments that make their own exquisite gelato—you might want to try a gelato in one place and then walk to another for your *caffè* chaser.

In an unfamiliar city, it's always nice to know where you can get something special at a reasonable price, without bumbling around for hours. So, go ahead, rub elbows with the Romani as they chug an ounce of espresso in a tiny cup on the way to work, or linger all afternoon over a cappuccino and gelato and soak up the local color. *Café Life Rome*'s recommendations and unique look at local history will make your next visit to Rome a little easier and a lot more interesting.

· 1 ·

TRASTEVERE

Physically, little has changed here in the last 500 to 1,000 years—you could be walking around a small medieval city. Originally a quarter of Rome "across the Tiber" or trans Tiberim, it was inhabited by foreigners, Jews, and marginal types of the day such as thieves and prostitutes. Eventually it became home to blue collar Romans, and today is a popular place to live with expatriates and artists. You'll find lots of nightlife in pubs, restaurants, and pizzerias on the weekends, especially in the summer when it seems that every Roman from Trastevere is in the street, along with most young tourists.

Bar San Calisto

Piazza San Calisto, 3/4/5
06 5895678
Open 6AM–1:30AM, Monday to Saturday
Closed Sunday

The locals refer to it as "Marcello's," and it sits on the Piazza San Calisto, right around the corner from Piazza Santa Maria in Trastevere. One of the more lively sections of Rome, here people are often on the street until early in the morning. In fact, during the summer, many Romans are just sitting down to dinner at midnight in Trastevere's numerous outdoor restaurants.

The Piazza and the bar take their name from Calisto, a deacon who reported to Pope Zephyrinus and administrated a group of catacombs. These subterranean burial places for Christians were located just outside of Rome because of the law that forbade burying bodies within the city walls. Calisto's job was to provide a tomb for every Christian, including the poor and the slaves. He was so efficient that he was made pope when Zephyrinus died. Pope Calisto I then enlarged the catacombs, made them the official cemetery of the church, and gave them his name. In addition, he founded the first Christian church in Rome, the original Santa Maria in Trastevere, in the third century, on the site of a secret chapel that gave refuge to early Christians. Pope Calisto I died a martyr in Trastevere when he was thrown from an open window into a well.

Marcello Forti has owned Bar San Calisto since August 4, 1970. He's the low-key guy you find sitting behind the cash register, watching over the till like any good businessman. He describes his establishment as "a bar with a family atmosphere. In the morning, the people from the neighborhood come here… to sit in the sun and socialize. It's pretty much the same in the afternoon. And then in the evening it changes… we get lots of students and young people and foreigners living in Rome because they feel at home in Bar San Calisto. This was more of a neighborhood bar twenty years ago, but now we also get a fair number of tourists. We have a philosophy of low prices and good products, and word has gotten out. They say, 'When you go to Rome, go to San Calisto. It's a mellow place and the prices are right.' It's important to make money, but

it is also important to be recognized for your business philosophy."

Marcello doesn't think it is right to charge a low price for an *aperitivo* at the counter and a high price at a table—so at Bar San Calisto, you pay one price. Period. "Treat someone well and they return. And even better, they send another, and another," says Marcello.

Word is definitely out about Marcello's gelato, the specialty of the house. There's no "secret recipe"—he makes it the traditional way, from the best ingredients: milk, sugar, eggs, fruit, blackberries, bananas… and chocolate. Marcello's chocolate gelato is a masterpiece. "I make it myself because that way I can be sure it's made right," says Marcello. "The chocolate gelato wasn't this good when I bought the bar. A friend of mine gave me some tips… then I made some adjustments to the recipe and started to make it my way. I was a cook for ten years before I got this place. With cooking, you learn how to create and adapt."

Former owners include a man named Broccoletti who sold the bar to a Signor Vendidozzio around 1960, who in turn sold the business to Marcello. There has been some kind of small business in this space for eighty years; at one point it was a *merceria* (the Italian version of a dime store), selling socks, T-shirts, shirts, buttons, and broaches.

Marcello comes from Gli Abruzzi, a mountainous region to the east of Rome. Times were hard when he was growing up. There wasn't much work in his hometown, so in 1960, at the age of fourteen, he came to the eternal city and found a job as a dishwasher at a salary of 20,000 lira a month—enough to live on. He took all his meals in the restaurant and paid 7,000 lire/month for a small bed. In those days, a pair of shoes cost 2,000 lira; a movie was about 100 lire.

"Little by little, I became a cook, and then I got some money together and bought this bar. I've been working in Rome for 40 years… in reality it's been 80 years because I work two shifts every day. I go to work in the morning at 5AM; go home at 12:30 or 1, return at 8 or 8:30 and work until 2AM. Everyday it's the same. The restaurant business is very, very difficult. And it was a lot harder before, because there was no *riposo settimanale* (the one day a week in Italy when a business has to closed). You had to work 365 days per year. Now there are also *le ferie* (holidays). But I can't take them because I need a substitute. Plus, if I go away on holidays, when I return there's even more work.

"The best approach to life is to stay detached (*distaccato*) but not indifferent. You need to stay calm. When you work, you work and when you leave… leave work behind. If you want to live well, you have to work. Work hard, sleep, rest, stay tranquil…"

Marcello is definitely a hardworking guy, which is probably one of the reasons he started a family late. His wife was born in Damascus, Syria of an Italian father and

Armenian mother; she speaks fluent Arabic and Italian. She and Marcello have a nine-year-old son, whom they hope will be interested in the business.

In addition to tourists and locals, Marcello gets an occasional celebrity. Luchino Visconti, the Italian movie director known for neo-realist cinema, used to stop by the bar. His films include *The Leopard* (1963), starring Burt Lancaster, and *Death in Venice* (1971) with Dirk Bogarde. Once many years ago, Gregory Peck was making a film in Rome and came to Bar San Calisto for a coffee.

At the age of eighteen or twenty, Isabella Rossellini, daughter of Ingrid Bergman and Italian director Roberto Rossellini, was a regular. This was long before her tenure as Lancôme cosmetic's spokesperson and her work as an actress in films such as *Blue Velvet*. "At that time, she lived nearby, and she was always here. We got to be friends. She was very charming… we'd joke around." says Marcello. "She brought me a poster of Mohammed Ali from New York. He was training for his fight with

Norton there... in 1973. She also brought me an Ali/Norton poster and a Mohammed Ali commemorative medallion. They are both there on the wall. I'd like to see her again. She'd probably remember me. I hope so..."

When Isabella's famous parents split up, she and her twin sister, Ingrid, and her older brother, Roberto, lived with their mother in Paris and then returned to Rome to live with their father. In both places, the children had their own apartment, complete with housekeeper and babysitters.

At the mention of Isabella's mother, Marcello's face becomes animated and he gives you a thumbs-up, as he tends to do when he agrees with you or something pleases him. He and his wife are long-time fans of Ingrid Bergman; they especially like her in *Casablanca*, which they have seen five or six times, and also in *For Whom the Bell Tolls*.

Marcello says that this is a good time for Bar San Calisto, Trastevere, and the *centro storico*. "The eighties were terrible. Lots of drug use... right outside in the street. Sometimes young people would come in here high. It was unpleasant. I'm glad those days have passed. It is much better now... much more tranquil."

Wander the picturesque, winding streets of Trastevere. Visit Piazza Santa Maria, which essentially remains unchanged since the 1600s, aside from the gray marble that was added to the fountain in 1692. Also, count your blessings and be happy you weren't visiting in 1598 when the nearby Tiber overflowed its banks and the area was under eighteen feet (six meters) of water. At break time, don't choose one of the high-priced cafés on the piazza. Instead, go around the corner to Piazza San Calisto and grab a table at unpretentious Bar San Calisto. Marcello's prices and coffee are good, and his chocolate ice cream, with a dollop of real whipped cream on top, is excellent. Interesting people watching, with a mixture of locals and tourists.

Bar Trilussa

Viale Trastevere, 76
06 5809131
Open 6:30AM–9PM daily

*I*magine Danny DeVito with a moustache, speaking Italian—that's Mario Bianchi, owner of Bar Trilussa. Raspy-voiced, energetic, and philosophical, Mario loves to talk about life, and Rome, his native city.

"I was born here in Trastevere, on Via Scarpetta, January 24, 1945. At that time, Rome was only about ten kilometers by ten kilometers… it was all countryside beyond Porta Portese and Trastevere. My older brother remembers when the Americans entered Trastevere during World War II. He wore this aluminum drink container strapped to his waist, and sold them drinks. After the war, Rome really expanded.

"I left school at fourteen and, at seventeen, worked as an *artigiano* (craftsman), making chairs and sofas. When a wooden chair is finished, you've got a beautiful, tangible thing… soft and comfortable. Inside, I felt good… gratified.

"I loved my father more than anyone. He always watched me play football… we were very connected. When I was sixteen, in 1960, Rome hosted the Olympics, and my father gave me a tie with the symbol of the Olympics… I loved that tie…

unfortunately it got lost. During this time, I was playing football with a group that was lucky enough to play in the Olympic stadium for two half-hour periods before Italy played Spain.

"It was a very emotional experience to come into the stadium with all of those people, some of them from my neighborhood, calling my name. We all have a moment of glory... that was mine.

"Before I was born, my father was a driver for a famous popular singer named Gianna Pedersini in the 1930s and early 1940s. She owned a twelve-cylinder Isotta Fraschini, the same car that Rodolfo Valentino had in Italy. When my father drove her from Rome to her large villa on the Yugoslavian border, there was no smoking and no stopping for the toilet. She was very rigid...

"My father always said that it's not money that makes a *Signore* (gentleman). It's how you are on the inside... how you live and think. He was a true *signore*. He wished everyone well, and he was very dignified. Always in a sport coat... even in the summer... in August... a sport coat and a handkerchief... like the older Romans."

In 1970, when he was 25, Mario bought Bar Trilussa from his father. It was originally owned by Signor Vittorio Tabutti, whom his father had known since childhood. When Signor Tabutti was ready to sell, he went to his old friend and said, "Why don't you buy it. You have three sons. You can live on the top floor attached to the bar."

Mario still lives above the bar with his wife, his mother, and his nine-year-old daughter, Martina, who coincidentally shares the same birthday as Mario's 27-year-old son from a first marriage—November 17.

Even though Mario never finished school, he reads a lot—a variety of writers: Oriana Fallaci, Pier Paolo Pasolini, Alberto Moravia, and, of course, Trilussa himself, the café's namesake. "Trilussa" is actually the pen name of Carlo Alberto Salustri (1871–1950), a famous Roman poet who lived in Trastevere. He came up with Trilussa by making an anagram from his surname. Signora Tabutti, wife of the

first owner, was a distant relative of Trilussa, and she and her husband dedicated the bar to him.

Famous for creating poems and sonnets in the Roman dialect, Trilussa never considered himself an intellectual but rather a poet of the streets, where he got his inspiration. He was himself a poor student who dropped out of school at sixteen. A few years later, a local paper published his works, and he quickly gained popularity. By the turn of the century, Trilussa traveled extensively in Italy, doing poetry readings in Genoa, Padua, Milan, and Reggio Calabria. He was actually a big star for the time—people liked his poetry and even more his recitations, in dialect, because he added just the right twist of wit, irony, and sarcasm. The poet often used animals, such as lions, monkeys, dogs, cats, pigs, and mice, to represent typical middle-class Romans and their foibles. He added another dimension to his work by illustrating some of his poems and sonnets in a political cartoon style.

Trilussa's popularity peaked between 1920 and 1930; after his golden years, he lived modestly until his death in 1950. During his entire life, he preferred hanging out in taverns with locals to hobnobbing with intellectuals in literary clubs.

In his latter years, he lived near Piazza San Calisto and Via San Francesco a Ripa. You can see a statue of the older poet in Piazza Trilussa in Trastevere near Ponte Sisto.

Like Trilussa, Mario enjoys rubbing shoulders with the common man. "I love my work because it forces me to communicate with people. I like collectivity… I like going into the stadium to see all the colors and 80,000 people… everyone there for the same reason. I'm a great talker… a real chatterbox. In fact, I had an operation to remove a polyp from my vocal cords because I talk too much and I smoke.

"With this type of work, you get to know life because you are dealing with all kinds of people… the good, the bad, and the ugly."

When it comes to the good, Mario has made many friends through Bar Trilussa: the Italo-American painter from Los Angeles, the doctor from New York, the gym teacher from Dublin, and the English girl and the Irish girl who stopped by for breakfast. One of them spoke a little Italian, they started joking around, and eventually became great friends with Mario. At the time, he had a small house on Monte Verde and he let them stay there. They wanted to pay and were amazed when he said, "Jackie and Connie, you've already paid with your friendship." They still send him a postcard and an invitation to London, every Christmas.

Over the years, intellectuals, artists, writers, actors, and musicians have traditionally lived in the Trastevere area. Some of them were regulars at Bar Trilussa. Domenico Modugno, the Italian singer of "Volare" fame, often dropped in to buy a bottle of sambuca. In the 1970s, when British actor Rex Harrison spent time in Rome away from his villa in Portofino, he liked to come here with his kids.

"A few years ago, I developed a friendship with Marcello Mastroianni," says Mario. "He was a very good friend of Sergio Severini, a doctor at Cinecitta, who now works in the hospital right around the corner, Nuovo Ospedale Regina Margherita. Both Mastroianni and Dr. Severini lived in Trastevere, on the Via del Arco di Tolomei. When Marcello got sick, he started going to the hospital to see his doctor friend, and often he came to my bar for coffee… and to have a cigarette… he was a heavy smoker. It's only 500 meters from my bar to the hospital. He lived in this area for about ten years, but I didn't meet him until after he got sick with pancreatic cancer.

"I was amazed at how he could be so important and so simple at the same time. He said, "Dammi del tu, Mario." (That is, to use 'tu,' the familiar form of 'you,' rather than the formal "lei," which is used to show respect for someone you don't know, especially a VIP or celebrity like Mastroianni. Mario had been using this form until Mastroianni asked him to stop.) Toward the end, he came to my bar one or two times a week. It upset me a lot to see him so sick. I used to listen to him instead of talking all the time like I'm doing now. He really loved Trastevere because it was a beautiful old quarter of Rome and he knew lots of people here.

"And then one day he came in and said, 'Caro Mario, I'm going to Paris to die.' Two weeks later he was dead." Mastroianni passed away at his home in Paris on December 18, 1990 at the age of 72.

Mario believes that certain people, like Mastroianni, live forever because they leave a great legacy that contributes to the world and moves life forward.

Mario, as you may have guessed, has many other observations on life, which he shares freely with people who visit his bar:

"Pursuing money ruins life, love, and friendship. Your fantasies become fantasies only of money. You lose your real dreams. And without dreams, you are impoverished.

"My soul, my character, my heart… I hope my son carries this forward. This is what is most important. Who you are… this is your legacy… not your money or wealth.

"I believe every human being should have a chance at redemption. For example, I've known a man since childhood, and he committed a crime. He killed someone and got 30 years in jail. In America, he might have even gotten the death sentence.

Anyway, after many years in jail, this guy is having a drink with me, here in the bar, and he said something very interesting, 'That young man who did that horrible thing 30 years ago does not exist any more. I don't remember him.' For this reason, I'm against the death penalty.

"I'm not afraid of death; I'm afraid of suffering. Death may just be the most just thing in the world. Because no matter how much money you have, you can't avoid it.

"Life is richer if you have a chance to grow old and understand a few things... even just a few things.

"After physical beauty fades, there is a more subtle beauty. That of the wise older person.

"In twenty years when I'm dead, there will probably be born a person with the same ideas, characteristics, with the same emotional interior. This is reincarnation. It is a similarity in spirit.

"My first marriage was a failure. My wife left me with a three-year-old son. But I say to myself, Mario, you had some good times, some loving times with your ex-wife 20 or 30 years ago, you can't negate that. There are a lot of stupid men who bad-mouth their ex-wives, ignoring intense moments, fantastic moments.

"In Rome, there is a great proverb... *The night brings consolation.*

"I like to get to know people, but not on the surface. I want to know what they are really like... inside... their soul.

"I'm not interested in a world where everyone is the same.

"I was in the hospital in `89 for a very serious kidney operation. I was there for a month. When I came out, I was reborn. I came to the bar... there was my mother, my son, and my friends... in other words, the entire world was waiting for me. The closer you are to death the more you understand the meaning of life. Looking back, life is beautiful."

Because he is so full of life, Mario was cast in a TV commercial in 1998. He was sitting in a chair in front of Bar Trilussa when an American director and a Roman casting agent noticed him. They were looking for a certain character for a Canon TV spot, and he was it. All Mario had to do was sit in the Piazza Navona and pretend to read a newspaper, then look up in the direction of a tall beautiful woman—though what really catches his eye is the Canon camera behind her. Mario says, "I had a great time. The sun was out. I caught some rays, and I even had an audience... guys on their *motorinis* watched me and laughed. It's fun to do something new. Have fun, and if you make money, all the better."

Mario is a philosopher; he loves to talk about life. It's rare that you get someone talking like this, period. Let alone in a brief interview. You'll find Mario either at the cash register or in his chair out in front of Bar Trilussa.

Bar Trilussa is a stand-up-and-drink-your-coffee-at-the-bar type of place. It's on the way to Porta Portese, the huge Roman flea market, and it's a good stopping off point while exploring Trastevere—located not far from where Via San Franceso a Ripa intersects Viale Trastevere. Specialties of the house are espresso and cappuccino, of course. Mario's English cousin and his wife, who live in Birmingham, come to Rome every year and always visit Bar Trilussa. And the wife always has three cappuccinos. "This is so good, I have to have another and then another. The coffee... the pastry... everything here is genuine," she says. A testimony to Mario's coffee.

If you want to talk soccer while you're in Bar Trilussa, make sure you get it right. Mario is Romanista (a fan of the local Roma team). And his barista, who has worked for him for a long time, is Laziale (favors the local Lazio team).

· 2 ·

THE PANTHEON

All roads lead to the Pantheon. This area around Piazza della Rotonda is strategically located in the heart of the centro storico or downtown area of Rome. It's not only a major destination but a neighborhood you'll undoubtedly pass through as you crisscross the old city on your way from the Trevi Fountain to Piazza Navona or Piazza di Spagna to Largo di Torre Argentina. And since you'll probably get lost, the Pantheon is an excellent point of reference.

Bar/Ristorante M. Agrippa

Piazza della Rotonda, 67
06 6794813
Open 8AM–1AM, Monday to Saturday
Closed Sunday

As a child, Renzo Di Giacinto played on 100-kilo sacks of coffee, stacked ten feet high. "They were my castle," he says. His father, who owned a bar near the Pantheon for many years, used to mix and roast coffee, buying raw beans from Africa and South America. If Renzo wasn't in the back making castles out of coffee beans, he was in front of the Pantheon playing soccer with the sons of local tradesmen, the butcher next door and the baker across the piazza. It was like that in the late fifties—the small business owners and the old families that lived near the Pantheon, Campo dei Fiori, and Piazza Navona all knew each other.

Then, in the sixties, many of these families moved from the center of Rome because the houses and apartments were uncomfortable by modern standards: there were no elevators or heat, and it was so dark that people left the lights on all day. The newer areas of Rome such as EUR and Monte Verde became the more desirable places to live.

As the families left the center, political parties, banks, and insurance companies quickly moved in and bought old buildings for offices, and tourists snapped up apartments. These days, the locals joke about the fact that few *Romani* actually live in the old part of Rome. Once again, though, the center is a very desirable place, albeit a very expensive one. An apartment overlooking the Piazza della Rotonda and the Pantheon is priceless.

Renzo still lives in "the neighborhood" on the Via della Minerva, just about 300 feet from his bar, in an old palazzo that has been renovated and modernized. He shares the building with two business offices and a woman from Los Angeles, who has an apartment on the top floor and visits Rome only a few times a year. One of his more famous Pantheon neighbors, actor Harvey Keitel, lives in a building nearby, and, according to Renzo, is very pleasant and often turns up at his bar.

Because the Pantheon is a popular location for shooting films and TV spots, there is frequently a production company in the piazza and many well-known actors have patronized Bar M. Agrippa—last week it was Nick Nolte. Renzo himself would be perfectly cast as a bar or café owner: charming, good-looking, and very Roman.

The Pantheon itself has had bit parts in many films; one of the better known is

Roman Holiday. In one scene, you see a shot of the Pantheon's columns, then go to Rocca's outdoor café near the Pantheon where Gregory Peck, Audrey Hepburn, and Eddie Albert meet, and Peck purposely spills drinks on Albert to keep him from spilling the beans. This funny scene is set in a café that never existed. The filmmakers dressed up the exterior of a slipper factory to resemble a Roman bar. The location is still there today, down the right side of the Pantheon as you face it. Look for the building with the sign that says *Fabbrica di Pantofole*.

"My father's uncle bought the bar next door to Bar/Restaurant M. Agrippa around 1913. He ran it from 1930 to 1937, when my father took over, and then it was passed on to me and my brother and sister. Eventually, I bought this place next door because I wanted to be on my own," says Renzo.

His father experienced life in Rome during the Fascist period. These were very severe times when bars were not allowed to stay open late, and everyone had to be off the streets early. People were overly cautious about their behavior in public. "My father told me that when he was in his mid-twenties, around 1930, it was winter, and he had a cold. He cleared his throat and, without thinking, spit on the ground. Some Fascist police standing nearby thought he spit at them so they slapped him around and threatened him with their nightsticks. He was neither a Fascist nor anti-Fascist... but that didn't matter."

A hand injury kept Renzo's father out of World War II, yet he was still "wounded in action." It happened during the period when the Americans liberated Rome and there was much celebration. An Italian law said that bar and café owners were not allowed to serve alcohol to soldiers or to people who were noticeably drunk. One evening in Renzo's father's bar there was an American soldier who had too much to drink. He was loud and obnoxious, so his father asked him to leave. This made the soldier angry, and he said, "Don't come near me! Don't touch me!" He pulled his pistol with the intention of shooting in the air to scare everyone, however, because he was drunk, his

aim was off when he fired—the bullet grazed Renzo's father's forehead. The American MPs were on the scene almost immediately and took the soldier away.

Renzo's favorite story about his father centers around a free breakfast. "This was a time when all the old restaurant and shop owners on the piazza were friends. It was a special kind of friendship. Almost like a clan. They used to play practical jokes on each other, which is part of the Roman personality. So they played this great joke on my father. One morning they put a big sign over the bar… way up high… that said today was a holiday and breakfast was free. My father was not aware of this. Everyone would come in, eat, and then leave without paying. My father couldn't figure out what was going on. After an hour or two, he saw the sign. All of his friends on the piazza got a big laugh out of this."

The piazza in front of the Pantheon, Piazza della Rotonda, has historically been a marketplace. Farmers and livestock breeders came from the countryside around Rome and as far away as Tuscany to sell sheep, cattle, and produce. They would gather early in the morning by the fountain with mediators, people who would "do the deal" and negotiate agreements between the buyers and sellers. This is where butchers and restaurant owners came to buy the baby lamb for *abbacchio*, a Roman specialty, and also where wine makers sold their *vino locale*, which they carried in small barrels on wine carts or *carrozze* from the Castelli Romani outside of Rome.

From morning to night, people would stand around the fountain in the center of the piazza and talk. For that reason, it was called *La Fontana della Chiacchiera* or fountain of chatter. This practice went on until ten or fifteen years ago.

Recent excavation work on the piazza uncovered ancient Roman pavement below the many levels of civilization and construction, which indicates that the Pantheon was originally 21 feet (7 meters) higher than the street level. There were stairs leading up to the entrance of the temple.

The first Pantheon was constructed by Marcus Agrippa in 27 BC as a temple to all the gods of Rome. Around AD 117, the emperor Hadrian decided to build a new and better Pantheon. Under his guidance the replacement structure was completed in AD 125 on the same site. It is considered an architectural masterpiece of Roman history and a marvel of design even by today's standards. The dome or rotunda, made with solid concrete (a Roman invention), was the largest of its kind until modern times. The outside of the dome was originally covered with drawings, highlighted at various times of the day by the sun as it followed its course. Inside the building, colored-marble walls are still illuminated by light that floods in through the eye or oculus at the center of the copula, which has a diameter that is equal to its height.

In very non-emperor-like fashion, Hadrian refused any credit for the Pantheon, instead giving it to the original developer, Marcus Agrippa. This is why you see "M. Agrippa" inscribed on the porch of this 2,000-year-old edifice, the only Roman building to survive largely intact. The Latin inscription translates to "Marcus Agrippa, son of Lucius, in his third consulate, made it."

Marcus Agrippa was a Roman of many talents. Born a commoner, he became the

trusted friend and lieutenant of Octavian, who later became Augustus. Agrippa rose quickly to the rank of general after numerous military victories in Persia and Gaul, and returned to Rome where he was made a consul. He then switched to a career in the navy—distinguishing himself as the only Roman admiral to defeat the masterful pirate Sextus Pompey.

Back in the political world of Rome, Agrippa was instrumental in conducting the 29–28 BC census and subsequent reorganization of the Roman institutions, including the reduction of the Senate's powers, which led to the strengthening of the imperial regime. After this, he was sent to administer the eastern regions of the empire, and on his return to Rome, he focused on civic affairs and improvements in public works. During this period, the tireless Agrippa built the Pantheon, constructed two aqueducts, built baths, and cleaned up the water supply. He also found time to supervise the building of roads, plan several Roman towns and colonies, and draft a modern map of the Roman Empire. This was one workaholic Roman.

Of course, the modern Romans are known more for enjoying life. There is a saying, in dialect, that best describes the Roman character, *"Ce piace mangia beve… ce piace poco lavora,"* which means, "We like to eat and drink, we don't like to work."

That's not to say they are lazy. Romans work very hard, especially restaurant or bar owners. Renzo's bar is open from 8AM to 1AM, and he's there most of the time, except for a short time in the afternoon when he goes home for a rest or a nap. He employs a few waiters, but staffing is an expensive proposition. "We have to pay a minimum of $10 an hour," says Renzo. "Then you have to pay *assistenza* and other taxes. So that $10 becomes $20. If the waiter has children, you have to pay money for the children. After seven hours, you pay overtime… 60 percent more. Also, every year, by law, you pay three monthly salaries in addition to the normal one. That's one vacation and two extra salaries. Also, after you work for me for ten years, I pay you *la liquidazione*, 10 monthly salaries or one for every year. It's difficult to pay all the costs, which is why some families sell to a *societá* (corporation)."

Renzo enjoys running his business, and he also enjoys his day off: Sunday. "I should stay open on Sunday because there is lots of business, but if I did I wouldn't be able to see my kids. They're in school during the week. Also, my friends have Sunday off. If I worked on Sunday, I wouldn't see anyone. It's better like this. You only get one life… you should live it well."

Renzo's perfect Sunday: a beautiful day in the country at his father-in-law's place, football with his children, and a big family meal. *Ce piace mangia beve… ce piace poco lavora.*

Bar/Ristorante M. Agrippa is a good place just about any time you're near the Pantheon. Start your day there, drop in for lunch, or take a break in the afternoon. There is a bar and limited seating inside, but the real reason to visit Renzo is to sit at an outside table and people-watch on the Piazza della Rotonda. You see tourists from every country on earth, locals playing with their dogs around the fountain, and middle-class Roman families visiting the centro storico (downtown) for a leisurely stroll and a gelato. Even in the winter, it's pleasant sitting outside because Renzo strategically places large butane heaters around his tables. Just about anything you order at Bar/Ristorante M. Agrippa is a winner—coffee is excellent and the plate of grilled vegetables is especially tasty.

Giolitti

Via Ufficio del Vicario, 40
06 6991243
Open 7AM–12:30AM, Monday to Friday
7AM–2AM, Saturday
Closed Sunday

The government in Italy is all the better for gelato—especially the kind found in Gelateria Giolliti, just off Piazza di Montecitorio. Palazzo di Montecitorio, which stands on the piazza and was completed in 1696, houses the *Camera dei Deputati* or House of Representatives, part of the Italian parliament. Often you see members of this august body in Giolitti eating its exquisite gelato and finding compromise where there might otherwise be none. Disagreements tend to melt away over a large cup of *cioccolato* and *nocciola*.

The Giolitti gelato dynasty began around 1870, when Giuseppe Giolitti and his herd of cows followed the French army from Pedemont in Northern Italy to Rome in order to provision it on its march to the aid of the pope, who was a French ally.

Later on, Giolitti went to work for the king of Italy as a horse groom, a very good job for the times. Unfortunately, it didn't last long because he soon took a bad fall from one of the king's steeds and was seriously injured. As a reward for good and

faithful service, the king gave him the first commercial license in Italy. So in a room under a convent, Giuseppe Giolitti set up his business with two cows, and drove his milk cart from Filettino, a small hill town, to sell milk and butter to the wealthy Roman families of the day.

By 1890, Giuseppe Giolitti and his wife, Bernardina, sold dairy goods, along with their soon-to-be-famous gelato, from a store in the historical center of Rome. There is a favorite story told about Nonna Bernardina's marketing gifts. In the early days, she would often position a table outside of the *latteria* with her eight healthy, happy children sitting around enjoying gelato and other Giolitti goodies. When neighbors and passersby asked how she came to have to such beautiful offspring, she explained that it was all due to the magic in her milk products.

A second shop followed in 1910, and by 1930, Giuseppe and Bernardina and their offspring had five *latterias*, including the present-day location run by son Nazzareno and his wife, Giuseppina.

"Inside the *latteria* in those days was a large refrigerator of marble. That's where they put the milk… there were only bottles. And in the old days people would come in and order a glass of milk… it was served in these big, tall glasses. We also sold good butter made from the best milk," says Nazzareno Giolitto, a handsome man who looks like a cross between Alain Delon and George Clooney. Named after his grandfather, he is the owner of Giolitti, along with his mother and two sisters.

"First we were a *latteria*, then little by little we equipped ourselves with coffee machines, the kind of stovetop coffee maker you find in the home," he continues. "After that, we got espresso machines, and we began serving more and more gelato.

"Alberto Pica's father worked for my grandfather, Nazzareno, right here in 1930. He worked at the counter serving milk and gelato, and then eventually opened his own place. (Bar/Gelateria Alberto Pica is also featured in this book, page 101.)

"Even though my grandfather was anti-Fascist, they called him *Il Duce di Via Uffici del Vicario* because he ran things in the neighborhood. One day a small band of Fascists were selling 100 kilos of cocoa on the street nearby. This commodity was very hard to find, and it disappeared so quickly, that when my grandfather arrived there was no cocoa... this meant no chocolate ice cream.

"But things evened out later on when he delivered milk to the American troops bivouacked in Circus Maximus at the end of World War II. He wouldn't take money from them, so they gave him chocolate, along with eggs and sugar, which he used to make chocolate gelato. At that point, he was probably the only one who had chocolate gelato in Rome. In the evening the soldiers would come by and crowd into the gelateria. Even now, older Americans will stop by and tell us they remember eating gelato here during the war. 'We knew your grandfather and grandmother,' they say. So first we served the French Army and then the American Army."

Nazzareno Giolitti claims that this type of work gets in the blood when you're not even aware of it, especially after it's passed down from generation to generation. As a boy, he was always in the gelateria, and when he was very young, he even fought mock campaigns with little soldiers that were, in fact, pieces of chocolate wrapped in red and blue paper.

"My nine-year-old son is interested in gelato," he says. "What kid isn't? Whether he goes into the family business is his decision. I am the fourth generation of the Giolitti family in this business. It would be great if he continued in the tradition.

"My mother and sisters take care of the sales and running the shops, and I work more with the production of ice cream and pastries.

"As for the future of a small family business like this, it's hard to say. You have to stand firm on delivering high quality products. And you have to be open to new ways of doing business... on the internet for example."

The Giolitti family is fanatical about the quality of its gelato; this means fresh eggs from Rome, fresh milk from the Central Dairy in Milan, and of course seasonal fruit. The older customers prefer heavier, classic flavors: nocciola, cioccolato, and crema, while the younger people like "gelato light" with fruit, less milk, and no eggs. The concern for quality is also apparent in another *specialitá della casa*—whipped cream, whipped the old fashioned way by hand, which gives it a rich, unique flavor and dense texture.

The other Giolitti gelateria, called Casina dei Tre Laghi, opened in 1960, and is still going strong at Viale Oceania, 90 in EUR. That year, too, the present Via Ufficio del Vicario location was expanded to include a larger second room with tables and chairs. Later, in 1977, a major renovation changed the look of all the interior rooms—wood paneling and softer colors replaced the white marble walls from the latteria days, creating a much warmer feel.

Giolitti has also expanded its business beyond the EUR section of Rome. "I opened a gelateria in New York with an American partner," explains Nazzareno Giolitti. "I stayed there four months to get the business established, and it went so well that after two months the Häagen-Dazs shop across from us closed and moved to another area. The partnership lasted a couple years… I took back my name because the quality was not what I thought it should be.

"I had a better experience in Denmark. In 1980, we started with one little gelateria in Copenhagen, and now we have eighteen… all serving handmade gelato. We have a contract with the owner. We trained him, and he's continued with the business and expanded it. It's called Bravissimo by Giolitti.

"The Americans have a different way of eating gelato. They buy it and take it home for later, so they want something that will last longer. On the other hand, Italians buy a cone or a cup and go for a walk. Häagen-Dazs, for example, makes a good product with good ingredients, and it lasts for a while in the fridge. The ingredients are much the same as ours but the sales mentality is different. Our gelato is made in the morning and in the evening it is gone… either eaten or thrown out.

"Forty people work here and 25 in EUR. We have six *gelatai* (gelato makers) in total, one of whom, Billy, is like a member of the family. When he was twelve, he started with my grandfather and he's worked for three generations of the family… he's very famous in our business. We make six or seven *quintale* of gelato everyday. Of these, we make 1,500–2,000 cones, and the rest we sell in other ways." A *quintale* equals 100 kilos, which means they make about 1,500 pounds of gelato a day. No wonder they need six gelato makers.

It takes a lot of people to eat that much gelato. Tourists, local families, and politicians scarf up their share, along with the occasional celebrity. John Travolta has been known to drop by, and Sharon Stone stopped in on more than one occasion. "Not long ago, she walked in alone, wearing jeans. My wife recognized her, and she told my wife that when she was studying in Rome she used to come here for gelato," says Nazzareno Giolitti.

The pope is also a customer, and orders gelato from Giolitti for his summer residence on a regular basis.

The pope and Sharon Stone—that certainly covers a wide spectrum in the world of high-profile gelato lovers.

Giolitti is not far from the Pantheon, Trevi Fountain, Piazza Navona, Piazza di Spagna, and Via del Corso. Whether you're on your way to or from these places, take a break over three scoops of Giolitti's finest. If you can't decide which flavor to choose, just cover your eyes and point. They're all good. Then settle in to the main room, knowing that this is the very place where, in 1964, key politicians decided on the President of the Republic. His name was Giuseppe Saragat. They came to an agreement over a granita di caffé *(coffee drink with crushed ice, popular during the hot summer), and then went next door to the parliament to make the announcement. Only in Italy do they decide the next president in a gelateria. You should also know that this is the oldest gelateria in Rome. When you need a break from gelato, try their excellent coffee and pastries.*

Caffé Sant'Eustachio

Piazza Sant'Eustachio, 82
06 6816309
Open 8:30AM–1AM, Thursday to
    Tuesday
Closed Wednesday

*F*ace the Pantheon and look to your right. You'll see the Via della Rotonda, which runs along the side of the famous monument. Follow it, take your first right, and you arrive at Piazza Sant'Eustachio and Caffé Sant' Eustachio. The café is often crowded six deep at the bar, which is not surprising given that it's one of the most famous coffee bars in Rome. Some even claim it has the best coffee in the eternal city.

Certainly the Ricci brothers, Raimondo and Roberto, would agree. They are the owners and their specialty of the house, *gran caffé,* a creamy, frothed-up, double espresso, already sweetened, is to die for. In fact, says Signor Raimondo Ricci, who has a nice twinkle in his eye and always wears a necktie, "There is a woman from New York who wants our secret. 'Do you put a little egg or butter in the coffee?' she asks. 'I can't live without your coffee… I'll pay you if you tell me how you make it.' I told her that if I gave her the information then it wouldn't be a secret any more.

She said she bought our beans and tried to duplicate them at home, but couldn't. She was desperate. I had to look at her and shrug. A secret is a secret."

Signor Ricci is serious about secrecy: He has a shield around his roasting machines so you can't see the exact mixture of beans. Part of the secret behind this fabulous coffee is its 100 percent arabica coffee beans—the elite of the coffee bean world from Costa Rica, Brazil, Columbia, and Kenya. Raw beans are roasted in a wood-burning coffee roaster the old fashioned way, in small amounts for 15–20 minutes at low heat, instead of using big, industrial machines that roast large amounts at high temperatures for 5 minutes. Wood roasting takes a lot longer, but gives Sant'Eustachio's coffee its wonderful and very distinct flavor.

The Italians tend to use more of the higher-quality arabica beans than the American espresso coffee blenders. According to Signor Ricci, it is difficult to find a true Italian espresso in America, even with Italian coffee machines and Italian coffee. "Espresso is Italian, like Coca-Cola is American. It's an Italian word. American espresso is like saying Italian Coca-Cola. There is no such thing."

There has been a bar at this location since the late 1800s; it became Sant'Eustachio in 1938 and has been in the family ever since (the Ricci bothers are

descendants of the original owner). It was recently awarded the Urbis Mirabilis, which means it's listed among the historical businesses in Rome that have been maintained intact for many, many years. When it first opened, it was considered very chic. Previously, all the bars had dark wood inside, but Sant'Eustachio used mosaics and marble, which was something new and different. People came from all over Rome to see the modern decor.

The business started with one espresso machine, and after a month, they bought a second machine because they couldn't handle all of the customers. At that time in Rome, it was the only bar with two espresso machines.

A collection of old coffee makers sitting on shelves lining the walls near the top attests to Sant'Eustachio's long dedication to the art of coffee making. Signor Ricci

says that only a small number of his 200 machines are on display. In the future, he plans to set up a small museum for the coffee makers, along with old tools and coffee roasting machines.

The bar has the same decor today as it did in 1938. In the entryway on the floor, you can see a mosaic of a white stag with a cross between its antlers, taken from the legend of Saint Eustace, who was born in the latter half of the first century AD. Placidus, as he was also called, was captain of the guards for Emperor Trajan and also a hero who distinguished himself as commander of a Roman legion sent to Asia Minor. He had a beautiful wife and two sons. Life was good, and according to all records, he was a good man.

Placidus loved to hunt, and one day while pursuing this favorite pastime in the forest, he saw a handsome, white stag with a cross of radiant light between his horns. Profoundly moved by this, he converted to Christianity, along with his wife Teopista and his sons, Teopisto and Agapito. This was the beginning of his troubles in the temporal world. Partly due to his conversion (some say he was also robbed), Eustace and his family lost everything and were forced to abandon Rome for Egypt.

While there, another misfortune struck: His family was kidnapped by pirates.

Fifteen years passed and power struggles resurfaced in the Asia Minor area of the Roman Empire. The Emperor Trajan sent soldiers to find Eustace and ask him to take command of the Roman legions and restore order. Again he was successful and returned the triumphant hero to Rome, where he found his wife and sons who, meanwhile, had miraculously escaped from the pirates. Soon after, Emperor Hadrian, successor to Trajan, learned that Eustace was a Christian and ordered him to offer a sacrifice to the gods of Rome. Eustace refused, and he, his wife, and two sons were tortured and killed by being put into a large metal bull, which was then heated red hot by a huge fire. Not a nice way to go. St. Eustace' remains are in a sarcophagus that resides under the main altar of the Sant'Eustachio church on the piazza, which also has the white stag and cross prominently displayed on the front of its peaked roof. Other relics of the martyr are found in St. Eustache church, Paris. St. Eustace is remembered on September 20.

There have been attempts by the media, and one American magazine in particular, to conjure up an intense rivalry between Sant'Eustachio and Tazza d'Oro, another famous Roman coffee bar near the Pantheon. Both are old coffee bars and both serve high quality coffee, but both owners will tell you that they are colleagues, not competitors, and that the rivalry is a fabrication. Of course, if pressed, each will also tell you that their coffee is a little bit better.

The Sant'Eustachio clientele includes a variety of people: tourists from around the world and famous visitors such as John Kennedy, Boris Yeltsin, Sylvester Stallone, and Naomi Campbell. Once Catherine Deneuve came in and, for no apparent reason, left a rose on the counter for the barista.

"These people get in line just like everyone else," says Signor Ricci. "Also, politicians, ministers, and senators come here. Sometimes they wait fifteen minutes for a coffee if we're really crowded. Right nearby is the senate… you can see the senate building from here."

Palazzo Madama, which is literally a five-minute walk from Sant'Eustachio, houses Italy's senate. The building was constructed by the Medici family in 1504 and named after Madama Margherita d'Austria, the widow of Alessandro de'Medici. Other famous residents included two upwardly mobile cardinals, who later became Pope Leo X and Pope Clement VIII.

Speaking of important people, Sant'Eustachio was on the itinerary of Henry Kissinger during a visit he made to Rome years ago for a meeting on Eurocommunism. Kissinger left the Excelsior Hotel, and, much to the dismay of his security detail, sauntered like a tourist down the Via Veneto to the Piazza Barberini, over to the Via Frattina, and then to the Piazza San Silvestro, where he had a ten o'clock meeting with President Andreotti. Afterwards, it was on to the Pantheon and around the corner to Sant'Eustachio. After downing a *gran caffè*, the smiling and relaxed ex-secretary-of-state gave a thumbs up, followed by the profound statement, "Very good, very strong."

According to Signor Ricci, young Romans also like Sant'Eustachio, especially in the evenings, which is truly a phenomenon given that this age group isn't known for hanging out and drinking coffee at night. Nevertheless, from roughly ten PM until one AM, they fill the coffee bar.

Is this the best coffee in Rome? When you're in the Pantheon area you should definitely stop by and make up your own mind. You have to be ready to wait, though, if you hit one of the many daily rushes. And, if you visit at the end of a day of walking all over Rome, don't expect to find a seat—there are only a few tables outside. It's good to remember that this is not a watch-the-crowd-from-your-table sort of place, but rather a stand-up-and-slam-it-down Roman coffee bar.

Aside from the famous gran caffè, Sant'Eustachio serves other specialties such as cappuccino, granita di caffè, and Irish coffee. And everything comes sweetened, so if you don't want sugar be sure to tell them ahead of time.

Tazza d'Oro

La Casa del Caffé
Via degli Orfani, 84
06 6792768

Open 7AM–8PM, Monday to Saturday
Closed Sunday

Owner Natalia Fiocchetto, a gentle, serious woman, says her grandfather was bitten by the coffee bug while traveling as a tourist in Brazil and Jamaica. After visiting a number of coffee plantations, he returned to Italy and started a coffee business. In those days, coffee roasters imported raw coffee beans directly from growers around the world. Tazza d'Oro, which means cup of gold, opened its doors in 1946, on the opposite side of the Pantheon from Sant'Eustachio.

As for the intense rivalry between Sant'Eustachio and Tazza d'Oro reported in the media, and one American magazine in particular, Signora Fiocchetto says, "There was never competition between us. We are a *torrefazione del caffé* (a coffee roasting house)… the only ones who have a license for roasting coffee in the *centro storico*. Our bar is here to advertise the coffee. On the other hand, Sant'Eustachio is mainly a bar. We close at 8PM and they close at 1AM. Many people have asked us why we aren't open late, too. I tell them I'm not interested in killing myself running a bar. The coffee roasting side of the business is the most important thing."

The coffee business is tough. To order coffee beans on the open market, you have to know exactly what you're doing, especially when it comes to arabica, which is the only type Signora Fiocchetto uses in her product. "Just because you use arabica doesn't mean you have the best coffee," she says. "There are many types; African is the best quality and it's also very scarce. It's much in demand because it's lower in caffeine. The higher quality beans have less caffeine. In fact, I reserve coffee a year ahead of time in order to get the best on the market; although, I can't always reserve the price. For example, if the dollar increases, I have to pay more." The raw coffee beans that she buys arrive by ship in Trieste, Genoa, and Naples.

Signora Fiocchetto's grandfather, Mario Fiocchetto, created the recipe for the original house blend. And, like every blend that Tazza d'Oro sells, it has less than one percent caffeine, between 0.7–0.9 percent. "Our coffee doesn't bother your stomach or your liver and it doesn't interfere with sleep. It has a strong flavor, but it doesn't make you feel bad," says Signora Fiocchetto.

Even though she studied architecture and art history at university, she has spent most of her life in the family business. Tazza d'Oro flourished because her grandfather was an artist with coffee and her father had very good business sense. Over the years she helped both of them and even managed to improve the flavor of her grandfather's signature blend. In 1989, when her father began having health problems, she became more actively involved in the business, and took over in 1994, the year he died.

It's very satisfying work, but also very stressful because Tazza d'Oro is a small business with lots of responsibility. She has a twenty-year-old son who helps her, and Signora Fiocchetto tries to enjoy herself, finding a creative outlet in her work.

"Coming up with a high quality blend of coffee is not easy. In fact, it is more of an art than a business," she says. "You constantly modify to improve the flavor or to replace a certain type of coffee bean. For example, during a part of the year, Costa Rican coffee is scarce. I have to substitute another type of coffee that has the same effect. Sometimes you have to mix two types to replace what is missing. You look for a certain body and taste… a characteristic. The blend determines the flavor and I always want the best flavor."

Tazza d'Oro uses gas roasters to cook the coffee slowly in small batches, which allows for more control and a better product. Big companies roast coffee in large batches with electronic machines that are extremely fast, but tend to overcook the beans. They even blend together three different qualities of coffee. Often, both quality and flavor suffer. All of this helps to explain why foreigners can never seem to duplicate the espresso they get from coffee bars like Tazza d'Oro.

The signora offered to share a couple of her secrets: roast the coffee a little more for the large espresso machines in the bars; a little less for the smaller, home-use machines. These are adjustments that a coffee artisan can make quite easily, however at the industrial level it's much more difficult.

Customers order Tazza d'Oro's coffee from all over the world via the internet (www.torrefazionetazzadoro.com), fax, phone, and mail. In fact, some people have proposed opening the business in other countries, but Signora Fiocchetto does not want it to turn into a huge commercial venture. She prefers to remain a small family operation and maintain the highest quality product. It's also a family business for the employees, who tend to work here for a long time—and then pass the job on to a son or a nephew.

The Tazza d'Oro logo—*La Seminatrice* or sewer of seeds, a tall, sensual, black woman scattering coffee beans around the world—reflects Signora Fiocchetto's grandfather's love of the Caribbean, South America, and the coffee it produces. You see this figure on the outside of the café and on its promotional literature.

A teacher from the Academy of Rome drew the original illustration in the 1940s, based on a concept by the signora's grandfather. Over the years, La Seminatrice evolved into a slightly different persona— her father used various models and actresses for advertising campaigns, some came from the Caribbean. The current order form features an Ethiopian actress and model, though the most famous Seminatrice is the original illustration found on the Tazza d'Oro postcard.

The Spanish tag line *El meglior do mundo* (on the sign outside the bar) was purposely misspelled by the signora's grandfather, Mario Fiocchetto, because it sounded better to his ear than the correct *El mejor del mundo* (The best in the world). In essence, he created his own word, *meglior*, by combining the Spanish *mejor* (best) and Italian *migliore* (best). Italians have always had their own way of doing things.

You'll find other tag lines on the literature and packaging: *regalare un sacco di caffè... acquisterete un sacco di amici,* which means "give a sack of coffee and get a sack of friends." Granted it sounds much better in Italian, plus Italians use the word "sack" like English speakers use the word "bunch." There is also *vengo da tutto il mondo... vado in tutto il mondo,* which means "I come from all over the world and I go all over the world," and finally, *aroma di Roma,* which plays with the word "Roma." This charming, old-fashioned ad copy captures the good will and camaraderie that is an essential part of coffee-drinking culture in Italy.

The signora's father even convinced the first Russian astronaut on the moon to do an ad for him. He was in town for a large exposition called the Fiera di Roma, and initial contact was through the Russian ambassador, a Tazza d'Oro regular. The result was a famous print ad with a photo of the astronaut standing next to a couple of Tazza d'Oro delivery trucks. The headline read, "You don't have to go to the moon for good coffee."

Before it was a coffee roasting business and a bar, the actual location was a shoe repair shop. Nearby stood a home for young, unwed mothers, and also an orphanage, which explains why the street is called Via degli Orfani (street of orphans). At one point almost all the streets in the *centro storico* were filled with craftsman and the names reflected this. Via dei Pastini, which meets Via degli Orfani to form the corner where Tazza d'Oro sits, is a good example. *Pastini* refers not to pasta sellers, as you might guess, but to craftsmen who make ceramics for the bath: sinks, commodes, and tubs.

These artisans had their own churches, a tradition that for the most part ended after the last war. If you go to the Torre di Argentina near the Pantheon, you'll still find a church, with English priests, where butchers and sausage makers have gathered since the turn of the century. They congregated in their own church when they came to Rome—much like farmers and shepherds who came to the Piazza della Rotonda in front of the Pantheon to sell livestock.

The best way to experience Tazza d'Oro is to stand at the bar like the Romans. In fact, this well-lit, pleasant establishment is designed to discourage lingering; there is a very long bar and very few tables. So plan to drop in for a quick sample while you are visiting the Pantheon or on your way from the Pantheon to the Via del Corso area. During different times of the day, you'll see wave after wave of coffee lovers crowd the bar. Tourists, housewives, politicians, clergy, backpackers, business people, and students gather at Tazza d'Oro for its famous caffè, along with other specialties such as granita di caffè *(iced coffee, crushed ice, layers of whipped cream) and* cioccolata calda con panna *(hot chocolate with cream). And don't leave without a couple bags of Tazza d'Oro coffee beans (they even have chocolate-coated beans). You also might consider a bottle of Tazza d'Oro's very own coffee liquor, "Aroma di Roma."*

· 3 ·

PIAZZA NAVONA
& VICINITY

First it was Emperor Hadrian's stadium, and he filled it with water and staged mock sea battles. Then in the 1700s and 1800s, the piazza was flooded during the heat of the summer so the Roman nobles could splash around with their horses and carriages, and cool off. The recently cleaned fountains give you a chance to see Bernini's masterpiece, Fountain of the Four Rivers, as it originally looked. Explore charming side streets such as Via della Pace and the neighborhoods near Chiesa Nuova, across Corso Vittorio Emanuele.

Antico Caffé della Pace

Via della Pace, 3/4/5/7
06 6861216
Open 9AM–2:30AM, Tuesday to Saturday
   5PM–2:30AM, Monday
Closed Sunday

Antico Caffé della Pace, or Bar della Pace as the locals call it, has three distinct personalities. "In the morning," according to Signora Daniela Serafini, the wife of the owner, "there is more of a family atmosphere, people who know each other from the *rione*."

Romans born in the old part of the city feel a very strong tie to their *rione* or district. The name comes from the fourteen *regiones* that the Emperor Augustus divided the city into during his reign. As Rome grew, some *rione* were subdivided; today there are 22, and you can still see the heraldic coat of arms of many *rione* located on the streets in the *centro storico*. Caffé della Pace is in the Ponte district.

Around noon, another personality appears, explains Signora Serafini. "The managers and business people come in, and often discuss contracts over lunch. A little later in the afternoon, it becomes a tearoom. Customers eat little cakes and chocolates with English-style tea, and we play classical music.

"At night, the atmosphere changes again. It's actors, artists, directors... the night owls. They drink more alcohol than coffee, and they like the music a little louder.

There's something for everyone."

As a magnet for celebrity types from show business and the culture in general, Caffé della Pace is the closest thing there is to *La DolceVita* (the sweet life) in today's Rome. It's also a launching pad for aspiring actors and actresses—they come here to work as waiters and waitresses hoping to network and be discovered, and over the years many have successfully moved on.

Caffé della Pace is also a hangout for celebrity watchers like Rino Barillari, the King of Paparazzi. He's almost as well known as some of his subjects and sells his photos to magazines in addition to being on staff at *Il Messaggero*, the Rome daily. Barillari, in his mid-fifties, is a restless, always-in-motion kind of guy who claims to have been stabbed and shot at, not to mention being slugged by Peter O'Toole and punched out by one of Frank Sinatra's bodyguards. During his career, 78 of his cameras have bitten the dust.

Originally, *Paparazzo* was the last name of Marcello Mastroianni's photographer colleague in Fellini's *La DolceVita* (1960). Fellini is reported to have said, "The name *Paparazzo* suggests to me a buzzing insect, hovering, darting, stinging"—an apt description for a group whose *modus operandi* is to chase and provoke their celebrity prey in order to get the surprise shots that earn big bucks from editors. *Time* magazine coined the word in an article entitled, "Paparazzi on the Prowl," and it soon spread to the pages of the entertainment press across the globe.

Fellini actually based his Paparazzo character on Tazio Secchiaroli, one of the original real-life street photographers who invented this aggressive and intrusive

approach. The irony is that Secchiaroli went from paparazzi to friend and personal photographer of the stars. His career followed the real "good life," which moved indoors after the release of *La Dolce Vita*.

Caffé della Pace has also had its share of intellectuals, such as the famous beat poet Gregory Corso, a dark, little man who once boasted that he never combed his hair. Corso is considered by many to be one of the big four beat writers and poets, along with Allen Ginsberg, Jack Kerouac, and William Burroughs, and continues to have an influence today.

There is a strong Italian connection here, which partially explains why the late Corso was featured on a 600 lire postage stamp. He was born in 1930, in Greenwich Village, of Italian immigrant parents. His mother was only sixteen at the time and returned to Italy a year later. Life was not easy for the rebellious youth: he stayed with his father for a while and was in and out of foster care, eventually serving three years in prison for robbery. While in jail, he discovered many classical works and began writing his own poetry. Shortly after his release, he showed his work to Allen Ginsberg—and the rest, as they say, is history.

Signora Serafini and the poet were friends, though she says they argued all the time. "One time he was drinking too much, making a scene. I couldn't permit that. We are very flexible and we accommodate our clients, but we do have a certain code of conduct. And many of our clients have become friends."

Corso had a penchant for outrageous behavior—one story relates an incident that happened in a restaurant in the North Beach area of San Francisco. In a very loud voice, Corso was telling friends about a recent trip to Italy and how familiar he was with the drug scene in Rome, when he was challenged by two policemen sitting nearby. As Corso launched into further and more vociferous explanation, there was a 4.7 earthquake that shook plaster from the ceiling.

Gregory Corso died in New York City of prostate cancer on January 17, 2001 at the age of 70. In his honor, the Italian government gave permission for his ashes to be interred in Rome's English cemetery along with Corso's two favorite poets, Keats and Shelley.

Years ago, Giuseppe Ungaretti, another poet, used to frequent Caffé della Pace. The Egyptian-born Italian was well known for his spare, intense, unconventional verse.

"Late one spring afternoon, about ten years ago, Robert De Niro came in, probably looking for a place that would give him some privacy. He sat in the back room. It was obvious that he didn't want to be disturbed. Of course, we left him alone. So did everyone else," says Signora Serafini.

Other visitors from the world of film and music include Al Pacino, Meryl Streep, Matt Damon, Madonna, and Prince. And once there was a party for Francis Ford Coppola, with a belly dancer specially imported from Egypt.

No matter who visits the café, Signora Serafini treats everyone the same, in keeping with the Roman philosophy of *vivere e lascia vivere*—live and let live. She was born in the neighborhood, rione Ponte, and actually met her husband in Caffé della Pace. At the age of 20, she was working in a large department store called Standa and would come here after work or in the evening to meet friends. Little by little, she became friendly with her future husband, Mario Serafini, the owner. They became engaged, got married, and now have three children, aged 26, 25, and 10. The signora says, "I married a man, a café, and his family. It's a beautiful family. When there is a problem, we have a meeting, and everything is resolved."

Mario Serafini has been the operator of this café for over forty years. He was very young when he became the third owner; it went from his aunt to one of her other nephews and then to him. There is also another café in the family—Mario's mother has been proprietor of Bar del Fico in Piazza del Fico since 1927.

Caffé della Pace sits on the bottom floor of the famous Palazzo Gambirale in what was originally a stable and a garage for the carriages. At the end of the 1800s, this area was rebuilt as a café. Over the central doorway to the palazzo you can still see the original owner's coat of arms containing a *gambero* or crawfish.

"With a business like this, there is always something to do," says Signora Serafini. For example, aside from the daily running of things, there are deft touches that help to create the atmosphere. She spends lots of time arranging and displaying fresh flowers, and she is always looking for things to add to the café to make it better— especially antiques.

The Serafinis almost never take a vacation. They don't close in August when the rest of Italy shuts down because it's high season for tourism and their busiest time. Sometimes they go to a house they own outside Rome to try to escape, but often end up worrying about what's happening back at the café.

When asked what she likes best about Caffé della Pace, Signora Serafini replied, "…the same thing I like about home… receiving guests. We do everything here with great care, with our guests in mind. At night, we light candles and create an atmosphere that is relaxing and beautiful. On Sunday afternoon, I play symphony music. When winter comes, I play *O Sole Mio* to exorcise the rain."

After visiting Piazza Navona, it's a good idea to stop by Caffé della Pace. Inside, Signora Serafini and her husband have created a turn-of-the-century ambience with chairs and divans covered in a deep garnet velvet, long smoked mirrors, walnut tables with marble tops, and a marble bar that looks like it was lifted from a Toulouse Lautrec painting. During the nice weather, sit outside at one of the many tables and people-watch from this prime corner vantage point. Specialties of the house include coffee, naturally, and an aperitivo *invented by the Signora, made with spumanti, bitter campari and grapefruit juice, called Hilary after her daughter Hilaria. She assures you that she named her daughter and the drink long before Hillary Clinton came on the scene.*

Bar Mister Blue

Via dei Banchi Vecchi, 131
06 68803742
Open 6:30AM–7PM, Monday to Saturday
Closed Sunday

Narrow, elegant Via dei Banchi Vecchi curves gracefully toward busy Corso Vittorio Emanuele, and you can almost picture the prosperous Florentine bankers sitting in their offices, which at one time lined this street, counting their florins. *Banchi Vecchi* means "old banks" in Italian. Originally, these bankers worked for the papal court during the Renaissance.

Bar Mister Blue is a neighborhood place, located on the bottom floor of a building constructed in the late 1400s. "It has been in business for about 80 years as a *latteria* and then a bar," says proprietor Giovanni Armillei, a hardworking guy who looks like he needs a good, long holiday. The back of the bar opens onto a *cortile* or little courtyard enclosed by very old three- and four-story buildings—it's like stepping back into Renaissance Rome. At the far end of the courtyard is a storeroom, which was at one time a stable. "When this was a *latteria* (small dairy), the owners kept cows back there, milked them and sold the milk and milk products... talk about fresh milk," adds Armillei. "And then years later, when the owners no longer kept cows, the stable became the office of a ragman... someone who sold rags for a living. The ragman probably had an agreement with the owners of the *latteria*. They sold his rags, along with milk, tobacco, and

groceries… in those days, you were licensed to sell everything. The old timers say his daily routine was to pass through the *latteria*, argue with people, and then leave."

Via di Montserrato and Via del Pellegrino come together at the intersection of the Vicolo della Moretta to form Via dei Banchi Vecchi. *Pellegrino* means "pilgrim" and these three streets were one of the routes the religious pilgrims took through the winding back allies of Rome on their way to St. Peter's, until Pope Julius II created elegant Via Giulia and humbly named it after himself. Still a desirable address, Via Giulia is one street over toward the Tiber. Before this grand new thoroughfare was built, the area sloped directly down to the river where there were sand banks, smelly water, and the occasional corpse drifting by. It wasn't until the late 1800s that the Lungotevere embankment was constructed to protect Rome from seasonal flooding and close contact with the polluted Tiber.

If Il Duce could have had his way, the area from the Ponte Mazzini on one side of the Via Giulia to the Corso Vittorio Emanuele on the other side would have been turned into a wide street, probably cutting off part of the Via dei Banchi Vecchi. Luckily, the Romani were outraged at the idea of tearing down the old neighborhoods, and Mussolini decided to cancel his plans. He did, however, successfully complete other similar urban renewal plans: Via dei Fori Imperiali was constructed through the heart of ancient Rome so he could see the Colosseum from his office in Palazzo Venezia, and fifteenth-century neighborhoods were torn down to create Via della Conciliazione, the grand entrance to the Vatican.

Further down the Via Giulia toward the Largo dei Fiorentini, at number 85, sits Raphael's house. Although he died before the house was built, the famous artist owned the lot, which he snatched up as the prestigious new street was developed. In another life, he might have had a successful career in real estate.

Signor Armillei came to the neighborhood in 1997 when he bought Bar Mister Blue. Previously, he owned a bar in Torino, worked as a night porter, and was a barman for many years in various hotels in Rome and around Italy.

"The Italian anti-Mafia unit is 500 meters from here on the Via Giulia," he says. "Lots of police and *carabinieri* come in here. Needless to say, I don't have any trouble in my bar. I also get locals, people who work in the area, and the occasional tourist. Sometimes older people who were born here and then moved out of the *centro storico* come in and reminisce about how they lived here and who used to come in…

"They say Totó used to come in here… this was about forty years ago." Totó, a very popular Neopolitan comic famous for his broad humor and animated face, made many Italian "B" comedies up until his death in 1968. Many Italians feel his importance as a comic actor is underrated.

Totó's photo is but one of the many on the wall directly across from the bar, a pantheon of Italian celebrities, all deceased. When he first came in, Carlo Verdone, a versatile and well-known Italian film personality in his own right, took one look at the wall full of dead actors and said "What is this…a cemetery?" According to Signor Armillei, the chubby writer, director, and comic actor has been in six or seven times since he's owned the place. "Verdone is from this *quartiere* (neighborhood)… born near the Ponte Sisto…600 meters from Via Giulia.

Another member of the pantheon is Edoardo De Filippo, a writer, director, and comic actor extraordinaire: the Italian equivalent of Bob Hope in terms of status. Alongside him is his equally talented brother Peppino, who teamed up with Totó for five very successful Italian comedies during the 1950s.

There's also a photo of Aldo Fabrizi, a funny, talented man: actor, director, cook, producer, and Roman. He wrote and directed the first comedy that paired Totó and Peppino, called *Totó, Peppino, e La Malafemmina* (1956) (Totó, Peppino and the prostitute).

Two residents of the wall are better known outside of Italy than the others. Massimo Troisi, nominated for an Oscar for his poignant role in *Il Postino* (1994), died of heart problems at age 41 shortly after he finished the movie, and Anna Magnani won an Oscar in 1956 for the *Rose Tattoo*, written especially for her by Tennessee Williams when she was well into middle age. Bette Davis called the larger-than-life Magnani "the greatest living actress I have ever seen."

Whether you're shopping for antiques on the Via Giulia, on your way to visit the Vatican, or simply poking around this part of the historical center of Rome, Bar Mister Blue is a good place to take a break. Grab a caffè *or a cappuccino (both are excellent). Look at Signor Armillei's celebrity wall. Soak up a little local color. There is something soothing to eye about the graceful curve of Via dei Banchi Vecchi—just walking down the charming old street has a positive effect on the spirit.*

Pasticceria Bella Napoli

Corso Vittorio Emanuele, 246
06 6877048
Open 7:30AM–9PM, Sunday to Friday
Closed Saturday

A little bit of Naples in Rome, and probably the best pastry you'll ever eat—that's what you'll find at Bella Napoli. The specialty of the house is the *sfogliatella*. It is fan or shell-shaped, with semolina, ricotta, orange essence, candied fruit, and nuts encased in thin layers of flaky dough, and has an incredibly light, delicate flavor. If you've never tried one, go directly to Bella Napoli for your first breakfast in Rome. If you are familiar with this treat, then all the better reason to start the day there.

The Arabs originally introduced Europe to the art of making the delicate pastry that is the basis for this treat, and a group of nuns near Naples ran with the idea. Around 1700, the convent of Santa Rosa created the first *sfogliatella*; the abbess named it Torta Santa Rosa in honor of their founder. This cake was much larger than its present-day descendent, which fits nicely in the palm of your hand—and it was probably a lot less appealing, since it used rendered pork fat instead of butter.

According to the owners, Bruno Barbaro and his wife, Linda, "This is the same *sfogliatella* you get in Naples because we use the same ingredients and methods. The recipe is not as important as the ingredients. You need a good ricotta… some places

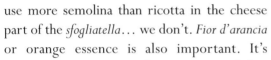

use more semolina than ricotta in the cheese part of the *sfogliatella*… we don't. *Fior d'arancia* or orange essence is also important. It's difficult to find, especially in its natural form, which is all we use. The oil is extracted from the skin of the orange, and then reduced through various procedures until it becomes very concentrated. We've always tried to make things the old-fashioned way. The traditional way. This guarantees a high level of quality."

Raffaele Portanova, Signor Barbaro's mother's uncle or his grandfather's brother (whichever way you want to look at it), started Bella Napoli in June of 1920. In addition to being involved in local politics in Naples, he was a mechanic for the Italian railroads back in its steam engine days. He also rubbed elbows with E.A. Mario, who wrote lyrics and music for the one of the most famous of Neopolitan songs, *Santa Lucia Luntana* (1919), which you still hear frequently, along with his popular World War I victory tune entitled, *La Leggenda del Piave* (1918). E.A. Mario is actually a pseudonym for Giovanni Ermete Gaeta (1884–1961). No one seems to know why he chose this particular pen name. In any case, do not confuse him with Teodoro Cottrau (1827–1879), author of the lesser-known Neapolitan song called simply *Santa Lucia*. Cottrau would often write at three in the morning, much to the disapproval of his wife, who eventually left him so she could get a good night's sleep. When an idea for a song appeared to him in a dream, he'd jump up and write.

Another songwriter friend of Signor Portanova, Afrontata Amario, liked to rewrite songs from Verdi's opera "Tosca" to include references to the *sfogliatella*. You could say there was a strong "*sfogliatella* connection" between these two men.

Anyway, one day, Signor Portanova decided to move to Rome and sell Neapolitan pastries, which were almost unknown in the eternal city. So, at the age of 48, he made a big career change and opened Bella Napoli.

Judging by his first newspaper ad, he could have also had a career as a copywriter in the advertising world. The advertisement, trying to get the Romani to try this new and unique pastry, was way ahead of its time—a tongue-in-cheek play on a single's personal ad:

Napoletana
Calda
Fragrante
Cerca compagnia

It translates to the following:

Neopolitan (implied female because of feminine ending)
Hot
Fragrant
Looking for company

Everyone thought the ad was talking about a woman from Naples, instead of a pastry from Naples. At the same time, he placed another suggestive ad in the newspaper:

La Signora Sfogliatella si offriva per una lira.
(Mrs. Sfogliatella makes herself available for a lire.)

"Signor Portanova died at age 97, in 1966. Everyday, he'd come in at nine and leave at five. After that, his sister ran the business until she was 86," says the soft-spoken, dignified Signor Barbaro. "My father, Ciro Barbaro, was next, and finally, my mother, Vera Portanova. I left my job in the bank after eighteen years to move the business ahead. I've been involved in Bella Napoli for twenty years, but only full time for the last six years. I have to say it's less tranquil here than in the bank, but certainly more enjoyable. And a much more complicated business to run than it was in 1920. I'm hoping that my nephew will take over after me."

Signor Barbaro considers Bella Napoli an important piece of family history, and part of that tradition is treating customers very well. They have always served a very diverse type of clientele—business people, locals, actors, celebrities; all are on the same level. For example, in a small, appealing brochure that Signor Barbaro uses to promote the business, there is a photo, taken in 1942 at the old location, featuring Edoardo De Filippo, the one called the Italian Bob Hope, standing, and his brother, Peppino, sitting at the counter—just like everyone else. Edoardo was a writer, director, and comic actor extraordinaire, who initially made his mark on stage with Peppino, also an actor, and eventually expanded his work to TV and film. Many consider him to be one of the greats of the last century, especially for his ability to portray the comic-tragedy of everyday life.

Sergio Rubini, one of Italy's most versatile stars, is another regular. Tall and thin, you may remember him as Inspector Roverini, the plainclothes Italian policeman investigating Matt Damon's character in *The Talented Mr. Ripley*. Among Rubini's many acting credits is Fellini's *Intervista* (Interview), in which he played the famed director as a young man. He made his debut as a film director in 1990 with the film *La Stazione,* and in 1998, Rubini also co-starred with Vanessa Redgrave and Gerard Depardieu in *Mirka.*

Frederico Fellini himself, and his wife, actress Giulietta Masina, used to drop in from time to time. Once, Fellini even complimented Signora Barbaro on her beautiful eyes. Another very famous Italian film director, Bernardo Bertolucci, of *Last Tango in Paris, The Last Emperor,* and *The Sheltering Sky* fame has an office nearby. "I would call him a 'regular.' More often than not he sends someone… an assistant… to get cakes from us," says Signor Barbaro. "He likes *caprese*… dry, with almonds and hazelnuts…a classic cake from Capri. If he accidentally gets the wrong cake in his order, he always says, 'No problem. This is better than what I was thinking of.'"

You could also rub elbows with Carlo Verdone, another versatile actor and well-known Italian film personality. The writer, director, and comic actor made his first short feature, *Poesia Solare,* with a video camera he bought from Isabella Rossellini. It was about then that director Sergio Leone of spaghetti-western fame came on the scene and produced Verdone's first feature, *Un Sacco Bello* (1979), taken from sketches he had written for a TV show called "Non Stop." Leone spent a night walking back and forth on the Ponte Sisto trying to calm Verdone's anxiety before the opening of *Un Sacco Bello*, which was a success and launched his career in film.

Bella Napoli has been attracting clients of all types at this location since 1962. "Before, we were near Fontana di Trevi. That was a location with more character but they rebuilt the palazzo we were in, so we had to find another place. This building was constructed in the late 1800s, by the Piemontese."

It was Piemontese diplomat Camillo Cavour and firebrand Giuseppe Mazzini, along with the dashing Giuseppe Garibaldi who undid what Napolean put in place when he annexed the French Bourbon-ruled south and named himself king of Italy (1796–1815). Their movement was called *Il Risorgimento* or "the resurgence." The Piemontese forces defeated Lombardy and then moved toward central and southern Italy. With the defeat of the Papal States in 1870, the unification of modern Italy was pretty much in place.

"When the Piemontese united Italy, they arrived in Rome and made this big street out in front called Corso Vittorio Emanuele. They removed buildings and neighborhoods… little houses from the fifteenth century… much like Mussolini did to build Via dei Fori Imperiali," says Signor Barbaro.

Mussolini had Via dei Fori Imperiali thrust through the heart of ancient Rome so he could see the Coliseum, symbol of eternal power, from his office in Palazzo Venezia, and also impress Hitler with this sight when he visited Rome. Il Duce, in cahoots with the church, did much the same thing with Via della Conciliazione, creating a grand entrance to the Vatican and tearing out fifteenth-century neighborhoods in the process.

Across the street from Bella Napoli sits the church Santa Maria in Vallicella or *La Chiesa Nuova* (the new church). This church was rebuilt in the late 1500s and became a symbol of rebirth and renewal following a period when many

Renaissance popes were worldly and corrupt. It was dubbed "new church" by the Romans, who still prefer this nickname. St. Philip Neri, an appealing figure from the counter-reformation and a priest known for charity, piety, and fun, made the rundown church his headquarters when it was given to him and his group of priests, the Oratorian Order, by the pope.

St. Philip Neri's flock, which came from the surrounding neighborhood, was a mixed bag of bankers and thieves (who had much in common), painters and prostitutes, printers and innkeepers, cardinals and church factotums. He contributed greatly to reforming the church and to creating a sense of community with his humanity, simplicity, and exuberance of spirit.

Chiesa Nova also claims its share of miracles—a fresco of the Vallecellian Madonna and Child on the wall of a hovel across from the church was the target of a neighborhood bad sport after he lost a street ball game in 1535. He threw a stone at the Madonna (some things never change), and the image bled from the cheek and neck. Later on, after the picture was removed and placed in the sacristy of the church, the very same Madonna appeared to St. Phillip in a dream warning him of a rotted beam in the rafters. Had Philip not replaced the beam, there would have been a catastrophe, killing many and causing great damage. Pietro da Cortona's fresco in the nave shows the Madonna holding up the roof.

Bella Napoli is more of a place to grab something than to linger. Don't let the plain interior or exterior fool you—remember, you are here for the sfogliatelle, and other wonderful pastries. Two sfogliatelle for breakfast could hold you through lunch. There are tables inside or eat at the bar. Coffee is also excellent, of course. It's not far from the Pantheon and Piazza Navona— en route to either of these places from Trastevere—and also near used-clothing stores and antique shops on the winding streets in the area across Corso Vittorio Emanuele.

· 4 ·

VATICAN

Even though St. Peter's Square and the cathedral are magnificent, remember that there is more to the Vatican area than the Vatican itself. When you tire of the tourist buses and throngs of pellegrini *(pilgrims) on Via della Conciliazione, turn onto some of the smaller streets, such as Via dei Ombrellari (street of umbrella makers) or Via Cola Rienzo, to see how Il Papa's neighbors live.*

Caffé San Pietro

Via della Conciliazione, 40/42
06 6864927
Open 7:30AM–7:30PM daily

*L*ocation! Location! Location! Caffé San Pietro is the only bar/restaurant on the Via della Conciliazione. It is just down from Piazza San Pietro, which means every tourist and tour bus on the way to the Vatican has to pass by. It might be tempting for some owners to take advantage of such a captive audience; not so with the Rossetti family.

People like the Rossettis give Roman hospitality a good name. They are incredibly kind and generous, and their philosophy is to go out of the way for a customer. This is reflected in the fact that they have expanded the café's public toilet facilities, along with those in their religious souvenirs store across the street, to help accommodate the large influx of tourists in the Vatican area. As a result, you don't have to race around Rome trying to find a john before you get in line for the Sistine Chapel.

Franco Rossetti and Stefano, his son, have even been known to help older tour group members who get lost. "Maybe, their bus left without them. Or it's raining and there are no cabs. We find a taxi and accompany them to their hotel," says Stefano.

"Sometimes tourists are robbed by pick-pockets when they ride the bus. This happened only yesterday to two Americans on bus 64 from the *Stazione Termini* (the main train station) to Saint Peters… an infamous route. When it does happen, we try to help by giving the victims the information they need and even accompanying them to the police station. The police have plainclothes people working the buses to catch these people."

"We try to treat tourists in the best way possible because it's the right thing to do, and because it's our best form of advertising. Even if they only come to Caffé San Pietro once, they eat well, people are nice to them, and they tell their friends," says Stefano. He knows that one could never create this type of good will working with an ad agency.

One tour director brings groups to the café everyday because the family is so nice and the service is great.

After being in the tourist business for many years, the Rossetti family has developed friendships with a variety of customers. There's the woman who works for the governor of New York, a famous Brazilian plastic surgeon, and regulars like the Brazilian ambassador and the Russian ambassador, who both often stop by for lunch.

Many clients also come from the Vatican Press next door, including Dottore Navarro, the *portavoce* (spokesman) for the Pope, along with his secretary and office workers. Other church officials often come here: cardinals and archbishops. In fact, there is a German cardinal who likes to eat by himself quietly and simply at a table in the back. "The Pope himself has never visited, or ordered an espresso to go.

He is a tea drinker… the Polish tend more to drink tea," says Stefano.

Caffè San Pietro opened its doors in 1775, making it the oldest Roman café in operation after Caffè Greco. The business was founded by a distant relative of the Rossetti family, Signora Moscetti, on the ground floor of a palazzo built by Cardinal Girolamo Rusticucci in 1572. Originally, the Cardinal had his mind set on a much larger building and tried to buy the palazzo next door, which belonged to a Swiss family named Stoker. They refused to sell to him, even though as one of the Pope's political ministers he had considerable clout, and after drawn-out negotiations, he gave up his plans for expansion and settled for a smaller place.

In about 1657, the Accoramboni family purchased the palazzo, and it came to be known as Palazzo Rusticucci Accoramboni. From there it eventually passed on to the Congregazione di Propoganda Fide (Congregation of the Propagation of Faith), which is in essence the branch of the Vatican that promotes Catholicism around the world.

The café passed from father to son, until 1968 when the Rossetti family took it over. "Our family business began over 100 years ago with my grandfather's souvenir store. It was a small store that sold souvenirs of Rome. We followed that with a hotel—Hotel Michelangelo—to the right of San Pietro," says Franco Rossetti.

The souvenir store, along with Caffé San Pietro, was in what was called the *spina*—a quarter dating back to the Renaissance that fronted onto Piazza San Pietro and stood in the middle of what is now the Via della Conciliazione, running from the Vatican to Castel Sant'Angelo. This neighborhood was the *spina* (spine) of the Borgo San Pietro district, and you approached the great basilica through a series of alleyways and windy narrow streets that suddenly opened onto Bernini's magnificent piazza.

The development of the Via della Conciliazione grew out of an accord between Mussolini and the Vatican. Both wanted to create a grand entrance to the Vatican, so in 1938 Il Duce demolished the *spina*, moving buildings and fountains. During this period Mussolini was on a roll: he built EUR on the outskirts of Rome (a new quarter with stylized monolithic lines) and also the Stadium of the Nudes in Foro Italico with huge naked statues, exaggerated because he wanted to portray the Italians as supermen.

By 1940, Palazzo Rusticucci Accoramboni along with Caffé San Pietro was reconstructed from original materials at the exact point where it is today. This is when Franco Rossetti's uncle took over the café. It had moved from just to the right of Piazza San Pietro, down the street to where there had previously been a hotel. At the same time, the souvenir store moved to its present location, almost across from Caffé San Pietro. The shop is called Domus Artis Roma, and it has expanded considerably from its early days—the interior renovated to create a number of smaller boutiques inside a larger store. It sells very high quality religious articles, souvenirs and mosaic art, and has thirteen toilets downstairs. The interior of Caffé San Pietro was redone in 1974–1975.

"When they reconstructed this palazzo, they found an ancient funeral urn and a Roman column. Under the soil of Rome there is immense treasure... like oil reserves in the Middle East... only ours is art. The government needs to recover it and improve the museums," says Stefano Rossetti. Anyone visiting the art treasures in the Vatican can count on a quality food, good prices and a friendly atmosphere at Caffé San Pietro.

A favorite Caffé San Pietro story, told by Piero the headwaiter, reflects the good will generated by the Rossetti family, even towards hardcore soccer fans. "It was the World Cup of 1994 when Italy played Ireland. There were about 5,000 Irish fans outside on the Via Conciliazione, singing and enjoying themselves. They drank 35 barrels of beer in about five hours... we ran out. They drank fast because the police had a policy of no alcohol after 4PM. But there was no problem with these people. They really enjoyed themselves, and were fantastic fans. Later on, we had to go to Piazza San Pietro to collect all the glasses."

Franco sums it up, "Beyond working and making money, our family has always been hospitable to strangers in Rome... to show them that Romans are very kind."

When you are planning a day at the Vatican, this is the place to grab a quick, Roman-style breakfast at the bar. The coffee is, of course, excellent. The Rossetti family uses their own blend. Lunch is also a good bet—the specialitá della casa *is a light version of Cucina Romana, and it's the only cafeteria-style restaurant near Piazza San Pietro. There is not much seating outside, but the clean, well-lighted interior offers lots of room. It can get crowded at lunch, but people move through the self-service line quickly. There is also another café in the family—Franco Rossetti's sister Mariella and her husband Antonio own a charming place called Caffé Accademia on the Via del Tritone.*

Gelateria Pellacchia

Via Cola di Rienzo, 105
06 3210807, 06 3210446
Open 6AM–2:30AM Tuesday to
Sunday
Closed Monday

*I*magine the chic Via Veneto of *La Dolce Vita* fame as an unpaved, country road running down from a series of meadows and vineyards that would some day become Villa Borghese Park. This is what Giovanni Pellacchia saw in 1890 when he arrived from Montefortino in a region southeast of Umbria and Tuscany called Le Marche.

He thought this bucolic setting ideal for a *latteria* or small dairy, which he set up on Via Sardegna, a street that intersects Via Veneto near the entrance to Villa Borghese. Like most *latteria* owners, he got milk directly from his own cows, which grazed nearby and were brought to stalls at the back of his shop for milking. In those days, Rome felt more like a small country town than a major city.

Around 1900, Giovanni Pellacchia moved his *latteria* to Via Boncompagni, a neighboring residential zone where a number of his good customers lived: Roman aristocrats, along with residents of newly constructed apartment buildings, and religious from convents and small seminaries. He thought business would be better closer to them, and he was right. The *latteria* prospered.

Nevertheless, people had to work very hard. In addition to milking the cows, which is an art in itself, he had to boil the milk in large cauldrons and then cool it

before delivery. While the process was not technologically advanced, it was hygienic enough to ensure a safe product. Eventually pasteurization laws came into being and a large central dairy or *latteria centrale* was built. Keeping cows out in back of the *latteria* became a thing of the past.

Being a flexible man, Giovanni Pellacchia adjusted to the situation. "My grandfather began serving breakfast... fried eggs and bacon, eggs and butter, coffee, caffé latte... he also sold mozzarella, ricotta... everything derived from milk," says Gianni Pellacchia, a charming, precise, and gentle man who is the grandson of Giovanni and the third generation Pellacchia running the family business. During this period, the early 1900s, the morning drink of choice for the Romans was not espresso or cappuccino, as you might guess, but caffé latte, a large cup of coffee with warm milk.

Business continued to expand, and Giovanni's son, Sante Pellacchia, and his wife,

Maria, became involved in the business. "Little by little they got refrigeration, although it was primitive, and began selling gelato," says Gianni Pellacchia. "The real boom or expansion of gelato was after World War II when cold technology began to arrive and fridges were much larger. It's ironic but the earlier primitive refrigeration actually contributed to the expansion of the *gelato artigianale* (handmade gelato) business because people could only produce small, handmade batches of gelato.

"Later on, Via Boncompagni was transformed into a *tavola calda*, and we offered a more complete menu with better service. It was a cafeteria, bar, gelateria…"

In 1923, the elder Pellacchia decided to open a second Gelateria Pellacchia, the current location, on the Via Cola di Rienzo in the quartiere Prati. This new, up-and-coming area near the Vatican was filled with middle-class Romans, many of them civil servants. Timing was good, and business boomed.

It was in this shop that Gianni Pellacchia says he learned how to make gelato. "Even when I was small, my mother literally raised me on gelato, she'd have me taste one flavor after another. Then I'd be behind the cash register with her or checking on the kitchen where they made the gelato. My father learned from my grandfather and I learned from my father. They passed down their techniques. We kept all the recipes from my grandfather, and by doing so have maintained the quality of the product.

"Today, you see many trendy flavors of ice cream… soy, celery, parsley, tomato. We make only classic flavors, with fruit that's in season. We don't use syrup. If we find good melons at the market, we make a melon ice cream. If the strawberries are good, we make strawberry. I buy the produce myself. For gelato, you need fruit that's mature, with a nice perfume. Last week the melons didn't have the right perfume, so there was no melon ice cream.

"The big gelato manufacturers use a base that's ready-made. They just open the can and add the flavors. We, however, handmake the base for every flavor with fresh eggs, milk, and cream. The egg has to have certain characteristics, the milk fresh... we're always analyzing the ingredients. It's a sophisticated process. And we don't use monoglycerides like the industrial manufacturers. They do this to keep the gelato soft.

"The secret of our gelato is that it's always fresh. Sometimes we make it twice a day, but never once every three days like some gelaterias. Salvatore, who works in the *laboratorio* (workshop or kitchen) has been with me thirty years. He *knows* how to make good gelato."

Gelateria Pellacchia is also known for rich, hot chocolate and has won an award for it from *Cioccolata & C.*, an Italian monthly publication featuring information and recipes on cakes and things chocolate. Again, Pellachia's classic approach—heating the chocolate very slowly in an old *cioccolatiera*—undoubtedly helped win the award.

Just as the Pellacchia family has passed its gelato secrets through the generations, it customers have also handed down the taste for this fine gelato. "There are Italians who come from other parts of Rome to get our gelato. Their grandfathers brought their fathers, and now they bring their children... they come for gelato and hot chocolate. We treat the little ones well because they're the future of our business," says Gianni Pellacchia.

"A number of tourists also find their way here—the majority are Americans and Japanese," he continues. "Our gelateria is very well known in Japan because it's featured in three or four guides to Rome. Every year, the publishers send their photographers to take new photos. The guides suggest that people go to a certain restaurant for the *tavola calda* and then come to Pellacchia for a gelato.

"We're near the Vatican on Via Cola di Rienzo which is not a tourist street. The tourists who do find us are looking for the real Rome… seeking out shops where Romans go. We treat them well so they'll come back, as opposed to other places that give tourists shoddy treatment… they look at it as a one-time visit.

"Sometimes, our customers voice their appreciation. The other evening a man came in and ordered a cone for 2,000 lire, then returned and ordered one for 4,000, and then came back one more time to order a large cup of gelato, at which point, he said to my wife, 'Complimenti, I'm Siciliano… I live in Milano and I travel a lot. I'm in Rome for a conference and your ice cream is the best I have ever eaten.' A compliment like that is more important than money."

Gelateria Pellacchia has had other fans, too, although some of them were certainly not the kind of clientele you'd want to cultivate. During World War II, the SS headquarters for Rome stood on the Via Boncompagni and the officers and enlisted men soon discovered the gelateria. As a result, in spite of strict rationing, Pellacchia always got the materials it needed to produce its marvelous gelato. Of course, those same supplies were used to make gelato for *all* of the customers, some of them members of the *partigiani* or Italian resistance.

Gianni Pellacchia also tells a story about the last Germans from the SS command to leave Rome as the Americans were entering the city. "They used whatever means they could to escape, private cars, trucks, anything. During this evacuation, two German soldiers came into our store, and they looked very severe. The shutters were closed because they were dangerous times. They were armed. I was very small, and I was terrified. They said go and call your father... he came out and asked them what they wanted... he was also terrified. They gave him a box of hazelnuts for his gelato and a tin of lard, which was hard to get during the war... and left in a hurry."

There was another time Gianni Pellacchia remembers being visited by German soldiers. It happened during a curfew, which began at six-thirty PM. His father had a small projector and was showing cartoons against a wall in the family home, when suddenly—a knock at the door! Two German soldiers on patrol saw a strange flicker of light coming from a window and stopped to check on it. "My father almost fainted," says Gianni Pellacchia. "He immediately turned off the projector, and when the Germans came in and saw what we were doing and that we were not spies, everything was alright."

"The war years were difficult. There wasn't much to eat, but it could have been worse. Thank god the Germans didn't bomb Rome. In those days, we ate everything, and nothing. There was also the problem of getting cooking gas, so when we found a newspaper, we would wet it, roll it up, dry it, and then light it to cook pasta or eggs. Most things, like flour or grain, we got on the black market, or sometimes we'd look in the countryside.

"I remember eating some small, dry biscuits we got from the Germans. You put them in water and they swelled up, like a sponge.

"When the Americans entered Rome on Via Veneto," he continues, "my older brother and I went to watch. There was this moment of euphoria... they gave us chocolate and Lifesavers. Some of them stayed at the Hotel Excelsior and played ping-pong. It was the first time I had ever seen anyone play ping-pong... around 1945. I was maybe 6 or 7, and I would stop in front of the long window with a view into the room where the ping-pong table was. I'd watch the soldiers play for hours. It was an incredible thing for me. Another first was popcorn. There was a popcorn machine at the American embassy and I used to go there and eat it as fast as I could, like a chicken.

"Abundance came with the Americans… they gave us powdered and condensed milk. The condensed milk was exquisite. I was going to school on the Via Boncompagni and the priests who were in charge got some of this condensed milk and they'd mix it with water and serve it to us in aluminum cups every morning before we began our lessons.

"The shop on Via Boncompagni was 100 meters from the American Embassy. We made gelato for the people who worked there and we developed a great rapport with them. Finally, after years of living in fear of the SS, these were good times for us."

Until recently, the Pellacchias had a memento from those last days of the war. Americans set up artillery in the *galoppatoio* (riding track) of the Villa Borghese and shelled the fleeing Germans. The family retrieved five or six spent cartridge cases, which Gianni Pellacchia's mother used as flower vases for years—a modern version of turning swords into plowshares.

After spending time in Piazza San Pietro, which is filled with tourists and pellegrini *(pilgrims) from every country on earth, you need to visit an area where the regular Romani hang out. Follow Via Cola di Rienzo, which runs down from Piazza di Risorgimento near the Vatican, to Gelateria Pellacchia at number 105. Grab a table outside, relax, and order a combo from the specialties of the house:* vaniglia, caffé, cioccolato, nocciola, *or* zabaglione *gelato. Better yet, try them all—that way you'll know for sure which one you like best. In between flavors, clear your palate with an excellent espresso. Gianni Pellacchia will be there. He almost always is, because, he says, "Work takes up most of my time, especially in the summer. We close late. I get to bed at four, then I'm up at nine and I return to the store to take care of problems."*

Remember to pick up your free souvenir postcard with its charming, stylized pastel of the gelateria by Roman artist and gelateria regular Giovanni Antoci.

ISC·TVDERT

· 5 ·

GHETTO & CAMPIDOGLIO

These two areas of Rome are like neighbors who constantly rub elbows with each other: if you visit one, you might as well visit the other. The city's Jewish population has lived in the ghetto area continuously for over a thousand years—hard to believe that at one time 5,000 Jews crowded into its very small number of square blocks. Wander through the side streets of the ghetto and eventually you come to Via Teatro Marcello. Michelangelo's stunning Piazza di Campidoglio is right up the street.

Antico Caffé del Teatro Marcello

Via del Teatro Marcello, 42
06 6785451
Open 5AM–Midnight, daily

Antico Caffé del Teatro Marcello sits on a street that didn't exist until the 1930s, when Benito Mussolini, in his infinite wisdom, decided that the center of Rome needed a number of wide roads. So, he cut Via dei Fori Imperiali through the heart of ancient Rome in the Forum area and built Via del Teatro Marcello on top of charming Piazza Montanara near Capitoline hill. Il Duce thought that these new roads would isolate and showcase the Roman ruins and also help the Romani get where they were going faster. One of the results is the endless stream of traffic on the Via del Teatro Marcello. (Luckily the war distracted him before he got too far along with his plans for civic improvement.)

"Caffé del Teatro Marcello has been in the family for 120 years...we've also had a business license for 120 years," says owner Mariastella Barberi. The first half of the café's life was spent on the Piazza Montanara, a large square with a beautiful fountain. The word *montanara* means "mountaineer" and refers to the peasants from the mountains outside of Rome, who gathered in the piazza 200 years ago to do their shopping after selling cattle in nearby *Campo Vaccino* or "cattle field." The Campo Vaccino cattle market was actually on the site of the Roman Forum, which lay partially buried for centuries until the area was excavated in the late 1800s.

When the Fascists rebuilt the Teatro Marcello area, many homes were torn down and Piazza Montanara disappeared, its fountain moved to the front of Palazzo Lancelotti. Caffé del Teatro Marcello managed to survive, more or less where it was, though suddenly it overlooked Mussolini's brand new street instead of the beautiful piazza.

Signora Barberi, a diminutive woman with red hair, says, "My grandfather opened the business on Piazza Montanara selling only cigars and liqueur. Then after a few years, he bought a coffee machine and began serving coffee. Little by little, it was transformed into a bar. He handed down this tradition to my father, Ernesto... the youngest of eight children. My father died in 1995, at the age of 87... a seventh generation Roman. He wrote a book on this area called *Ricordi di Piazza* (Memories of the Piazza), and he personally photographed many things that were demolished and rebuilt.

"My mother Elena Bruni Barberi was born in Boston 83 years ago and came to Italy when she was a girl. After she got married, she always worked in the bar. She is also a famous cat lover... *a gattara*. Six or seven years ago, the Italian TV stations and newspapers and also the *New York Times* came to interview the American cat lover of Rome. They wanted to talk to her because she feeds thirty stray cats at four every morning near her home in the Monte Verde section of Rome.

"I'm the third generation in the family business, and I hope it continues with my son, who's 23. His name is Ernesto, just like my father. He's beginning to work here, but not like I do. I began when I was 13, and I'm now 54... no vacations... without stopping. It's hard work. I start at 4:30 in the morning. I turn on the lights... make the cornetti, cakes, sandwiches... prep for the whole day... and

finish at midnight... seventeen hours every day. Day after day. It's a very tiring business. Many of the family bars disappear because no one in the family carries it on. You can only do it if you love it."

In the old days, all of the café's clients were Romans, who Signora Barberi describes as "sincere, genuine people, but very loud. There aren't many true Romans anymore. In recent years the customers don't seem to smile as much as before. In the old days, they were nicer, less demanding." Today, a variety of Italians and tourists come here, including well-known politicians and writers.

Among this latter group is the signora's good friend, Barbara Palombelli, who, in addition to writing for *La Repubblica*, a major Italian newspaper, is a radio and TV journalist, and also happens to be the wife of Francesco Rutelli, the photogenic ex-mayor of Rome (he resigned on January 8, 2001) and an architect and town planner. They are the Bill and Hillary of Rome—both have high-profile careers and are relatively young. Palombelli dedicated her recent book *C'era una Ragazza* to Signora Barberi.

Another "regular" is the writer Carmen Moravia, the Spanish-born wife of Alberto Moravia, a Roman novelist and major literary figure of the twentieth century (he died of a cerebral hemorrhage in 1990). There was a more than a 40-year age gap between the two. Carmen Moravia's latest book entitled, *Finalmente Ti Scrivo* (Finally, I'm Writing to You), is about their ten-year relationship. "She is a close friend of mine. She comes here every morning for coffee," says Signora Barberi.

Oscar Luigi Scalfaro, president of the Italian Republic from 1992 until 1999, dropped in with his staff one Sunday to have coffee. It made Signora Barberi very nervous to have such an important politician in her café, but she said he put her at ease because he was very charming. He even complimented her on the fact that in her establishment when he ordered a *spremuta* (fresh squeezed grapefruit or orange juice), he got a *spremuta*; whereas in many other bars he visits, he gets a *succo di frutta* (juice from a can). It's the little things that count.

Enrico Berlinguer, secretary general of the Italian communist party from 1972–1984, used to come here for his coffee. Unlike the communists that many Americans feared were hiding under their sofas, he supported NATO and condemned the Soviet invasion of Afghanistan. Former communist party headquarters were in the neighborhood on Via delle Botteghe Oscure.

Visiting the Forum, Campidoglio, the or Ghetto? You're close to Caffé del Teatro Marcello. Stop by for the specialties of the house: espresso (or caffé, as the Italians say) and cappuccino, along with homemade sandwiches and cornetti. While you're in the area, go see what's left of the Teatro Marcello, just down from the café. Originally built by Augustus and dedicated to his nephew Marcellus, it held 14,000 spectators. In the 1500s it was transformed into a palace for the Savelli family, and then later became the Palazzo Orsini. Today the palazzo contains a number of very upscale apartments.

Bar/Gelateria Alberto Pica

Via della Seggiola, 12
06 6868405
Open 8AM–1:30AM, Monday to Saturday
Closed Sunday

Alberto Pica is a man on a mission—to promote fresh, high quality gelato or *gelato artigianale*. In addition to owning a bar/gelateria, he is *Presidente del Associazione Esercenti Latterie Bar Gelaterie Pubblici Esercizi e Similari di Roma e Provincia*. In a few words this means president of the Bar, Latteria, and Gelateria Owners' Association for the Rome area. And if that's not enough, he is also president of the Italian Association of Gelaterie Artigianale, a group that lets you hang out their coveted plaque with the big "G" if your gelato passes muster.

Signor Pica keeps a grueling schedule. "Early in the morning, I come here with my wife, Maria, and we make the gelato," he says. "In the afternoon, I go to my office at the association and deal with the problems of the bars and gelaterie of Rome. Then, in the evening, I go back to my business." It's the same schedule six days a week for this wiry, little man who has the energy of half a dozen people.

"We have 5,900 associates or members. Every year we meet and elect a president... someone who is truly committed. It's an honorary title without pay, but I love doing it," explains Signor Pica.

"In Rome and the surrounding area, there are 8,500 bars and cafés, 5,000 restaurants... 100,000 stores. More shops, including bars and restaurants, are in Rome than in the state of New York and Washington combined.

"Rome is a tourist city that lives off this activity, so there's a store every 100 meters. Too many, really. Those with a history and a good product tend to flourish—for example, restaurants in Trastevere that feature *la cucina Romana*, or bars that offer traditional fare, like homemade *cornetti* and pastries. Of the 8,000 bars in Rome, there are about 1,000 like this... they've been around for a long time and are very experienced. They know what they're doing.

"For the most part, they use this formula, which is my formula: give the public good products... *sano, genuino* (healthy, genuine)... be polite and smile, and always treat people well."

Signor Pica is a fanatic about Italian gelato, which is undoubtedly the best ice cream in the world. According to one school of gelato folklore, it all began when Nero sent his slaves into the mountains to collect snow and ice, which he then mixed with chopped fruit and honey to create the first frozen dessert—a distant cousin of today's snow cone. The ice and snow were preserved in a wood and grass container and stored it in a cool, protected area until the emperor and his cronies were ready for a cold treat during Rome's sweltering summer. Along these lines, the Egyptians and Macedonians are said to have created their own cool dessert with semi-frozen fruit juice.

Another theory holds that Marco Polo started the gelato ball rolling in the late

1200s when he returned from China with recipes for the frozen water ices or sorbet that had been consumed in the Far East for thousands of years. It's also claimed that sorbet came to Sicily via the Arabs who learned the secret of freezing water with different salt mixtures from their contact with India. Probably more to the point is that gelato, as we know it, evolved into its present state from a number of sources.

Gelato folklore continues with the famed Italian gelato makers of the Renaissance, and the story of Signor Buontalenti, cook and pastry maker for Cosimo I of the powerful Medici family, who got the idea to flavor cream with citrus fruit and then refrigerate it—which gets us very close to modern gelato. When Catherine de'Medici went to France in 1533 to marry the Duc d'Orleans, she took her Italian chefs and this magical dish with her. From there, it probably traveled to England with a French chef who worked for King Charles I; his majesty was so smitten with this cold, creamy sweet that he offered the chef 500 pounds a year for life to keep the recipe secret from the nobility.

Signor Pica is part of this gelato tradition, as was his father, Antonio Pica. "He worked for Nazzareno Giolitti of the famous Gelateria Giolitti, near the Pantheon. And eventually, he got his own place," he says. "There has always been a bar or café or gelateria in the family, and from the time I was a boy, we were always making gelato. In 1960, we came here… to number 12, Via della Seggiola. The business has been in existence since 1911, and the original owner was Signor Zitelli, a *lattaio* (a dairyman), who came from Le Marche, the region southeast of Umbria and Tuscany. He had four cows that grazed on the banks of the Tiber where the *Palazzo di Giustizia* (Palace of Justice) and the Lungotevere are today. In those days the area was a meadow that sloped down to the river. At night the cows came to the back of the store, and they were milked. Besides being used for ice cream, the milk was sold to the public. This was a Jewish area… the synagogue is about 300 meters away on Lungotevere Cenci."

Between Gelateria Alberto Pica and the Tiber sits an ornate monolith called the Palace of Justice, containing, among other things, the Appellate Court, Criminal Court, and Civil Tribunal. It's hard to imagine a small herd of cows standing in its place, but that was the situation until construction began in 1913. Financial problems related to World War I suspended building until 1923, when the Fascists finally completed the project. In the meantime, Signor Zitelli's cows probably adapted nicely (Italian cows are much like Italians) and grazed around the piles of material on the construction site.

"The residents of the ghetto called this place *La Latteria dello Stufato* (the Dairy of Stew), because in those days there were no electric or gas appliances," continues Signor Pica. "Signor Zitelli had a wood or coal-fired stove with big pots of coffee, milk, and chocolate on top, like pots of stew. This heated the inside of the store, and the women came to drink caffè, caffè latte, and *cioccolata calda* (hot chocolate) on cold winter days because it was nice and warm inside… warmer than their homes. In the morning they drank coffee and milk or what we now call cappuccino… in

big cups, and they would dunk a big piece of whole wheat bread into the coffee.

"It started out as a *latteria*, developed into a bar, and then became a bar/gelateria. In the summer, we serve 100 flavors of gelato.

"Personally, I'm an *appassionato* of gelato… I like to make it and I love to eat it. When I travel around Italy with my colleagues as president of the association, I don't eat lunch or dinner. I just eat gelato… *cioccolato*… *zabaglione*… *fragole*… *limone*…I love it all.

"Often when I return here in the evening after working at the association office, I make myself two cones for dinner. Some of this and some of that."

Given this kind of diet, Signor Pica should weigh about 300 pounds. The reason he doesn't is simple—a small scoop of chocolate gelato, approximately 100 grams, contains 175–177 calories, and a scoop of fresh fruit-flavored gelato has 120–130 calories. Compare this to 100 grams of pasta at 450 calories, pizza with tomatoes at 247, or salami at 460 calories. Hard to believe, but true.

Who comes to eat Alberto Pica's gelato? A variety of people, including tourists, locals, and politicians from the Palace of Justice next door. Carlo Verdone, a popular comic actor, often drops by for a large cup of his favorite—*crema cioccolato*. Another well-known Italian actor, Carlo Delle Piane, lived upstairs for years in a room that has now become part of the gelateria. Delle Piane, born in 1936, was a child actor who began his career at age eleven in a film called *Cuore* (1947) with Vittorio di Sica, and for many years was confined to comic roles because of his large nose. (His nickname was *pecorino*, or sheep nose.) Eventually, he won a Leone d'Oro at the Venice film festival for a serious role in

Regalo di Natale (1986). He also had a part in *The Name of the Rose* (1986) and directed Brooke Shields in *Un Amore Americano* (1992), which may have been seen by three people outside of Italy.

Romans come from all over the *centro storico* to Gelateria Alberto Pica. It's especially busy during the summer when it sometimes stays open until 3AM. In the late evening, the city cools down to a habitable temperature, and it seems almost every ambulatory Roman is on the street eating gelato and enjoying life.

It's hard to say who in the Pica family is most interested in maintaining the gelato tradition. Claudio, Signor Pica's son, helps out in the association office, and his daughter, Roberta, works in the gelateria. His other daughter, Evalina, has eleven-year-old twins named Loriana and Ricardo who are very eager.

They said to their grandfather, "Grandpa, teach us how to make gelato. When you're old, we'll start making the gelato, and where it says 'Alberto Pica' on the sign, we'll put 'Ricardo and Loriana.'"

Signor Pica replied, "First learn how to make gelato. When you make good gelato, we'll see. We'll do a gelato test."

Gelateria Alberto Pica is just across the river from Trastevere, right around the corner from the Ghetto area, and within walking distance of the Forum and the Victor Emmanuel monument. Check out the long, gleaming display case with more gelato flavors than you thought possible. Whatever your choice, you can't go wrong, but just for something different try the very special riso alla panna—*with little pieces of* al dente *arborio rice and cream. This is a favorite of the ex-president Giulio Andreotti, probably the highest-profile, most contro-versial political figure in modern Italy. You may also want to sample the gelato called* ai petali di rose, *flavored with rose petals from Signor Pica's terrace garden. There are plenty of tables outside, so weather permitting, you can enjoy your gelato. Be sure to complete your experience with an excellent espresso or cappuccino.*

Vezio's or Bla Bla Bar

Via dei Delfini, 23
06 6786036
Open 7AM–8:30PM, Monday to Saturday
Closed Sunday

*V*ezio Bagazzini presides over the unofficial headquarters of the Italian Communist Party (PCI), located behind the building on Via delle Botteghe Oscure that formerly housed the PCI. He has filled this amazing bar with photos, icons, and trophies from the communist era and is more than happy to show you around.

This bar itself is about 100 years old, and has been in Vezio's ex-wife's family for a long time. "Originally, my ex-wife and I were here part time because I was a butcher. Then we separated and divorced. My parents died. I closed the butcher shop and came here full time. That was in 1984... about the same time Berlinguer, the secretary of the Italian communist party, died. He was elected in 1972. Since then, I've been full time in the bar," says Vezio, an intellectual yet down-to-earth man, with a good sense of humor.

"The photo of Enrico Berlinguer is the first one of a politician that I put in the bar. Before I had sports paraphernalia and posters of Sinatra or Bogart... the legends from my youth. After the death of Berlinguer, I began to collect political testimonials, in particular... for the Italian communist party and then the international communist party."

The Italian communist party was neither Stalinist nor Trotskyite, but instead marched to the beat of its own drum (like many Italians) and abandoned all notions of dictatorship, committing fully to democracy. "In the late sixties, one of the clients in the butcher shop where I worked with my  father was Giorgio Amendola, an important Italian communist. He influenced me. Also, in those years of upheaval and extremism (*gli anni di piombo*—the heavy or leaden years, as the Italians call the period 1968–1978), it was not enough to be a communist, you had to be specific… which kind of communist were you. There was Marxist-Leninism, Maoism, and there were forms of Trotskyites. So I felt a need to join the PCI because it was above all the party that had defended the rights of the people against military dictators in Chile, Greece, and Spain," explains Vezio.

Vezio's family butcher shop was right near the bar and that's how he and Francesca, his first wife, met. The bar passed down from Augusto, Francesca's grandfather, to her father, Marco, and his sister, Maria, whose husband helped out in the bar during the day and worked nights as a typesetter for a newspaper. When Francesca's father died in an accident, the bar was rented out for a while, and then she took it over. In 1969, she and Vezio married, and after a time divorced. There are two sons from this marriage, one named Marco after his grandfather, in keeping with Italian tradition.

"My ex-wife married again a little later. I remained single until 1994, when I met Maria, my present wife who was a customer of this bar… it was like a bolt of lightning. She was a student and stopped here to get a coffee before working on her thesis in archeology. There's a substantial difference in our ages. I'm 59 and she is 35. But it's nothing because when we met, we were two adults, not an adult and a child. She was old enough to know what she wanted. And she's a companion, a communist, and a Romanista like me. (A Romanista is a fan of the Roma soccer team. In Rome there is a great rivalry between the two local soccer teams: Roma and Lazio.) This bar has yellow and red inside—the Roma colors. My ex-wife was Laziale… little by little she's become less active in the business… and we manage it now."

The regulars who come to Vezio's bar are like regulars everywhere: they feel some sort of political or sports affinity with the place—here, they're either Romanistas or leftists. In the last four or five years, there have also been visitors who are foreign tourists or Italians simply curious to see Vezio's collection. To most, it seems improbable that this sprawling, time warp of a collection even exists.

"Many of the things in here were given to me. It's a disorganized collection… no analysis or planning. Having said that, I don't accept photographs of people whose philosophies don't go together. For example, there is a photo of Stalin so there can be no photo of Trotsky," says Vezio. Joseph Stalin, dreaded and mustachioed Russian dictator from 1928–1953, and Leon Trotsky, Lenin's right-hand man, disagreed on the direction of Communism. Stalin wanted to concentrate on developing the communist order in Russia; Trotsky wanted to focus on worldwide revolution. After Lenin's death, Stalin's star rose, while Trotsky's dimmed. After he was expelled from Russia in 1929, Trotsky continued to snipe at Stalin, saying that his dictatorship was self-centered while that of Lenin and Trotsky was enlightened. Trotsky was killed by a Stalinist agent with an ice pick in Mexico on August 21, 1940.

If you want to talk Italian Communist Party history, you have to know the main players. Vezio will gladly direct you to their photos on his walls.

Enrico Berlinguer, the first communist celebrity in Vezio's collection, was secretary general of the Italian party from 1972–1984. He advocated the moderate Eurocommunism movement of the mid-1970s. Berlinguer found himself increasingly at odds with the Soviet government and, in the late seventies and early eighties, supported NATO and condemned the Soviet invasion of Afghanistan.

Antonio Gramsci is the one with the thick hair and the little glasses. An intellectual and politician (a combination that rarely exists in the United States), he founded the Italian communist party. Il Duce did not like Gramsci and imprisoned him from 1926–1937. Soon after his release, he died of poor health in a Rome hospital. Anti-Stalinist Gramsci was considered one of the most important Marxist intellectuals of this century. While incarcerated, Gramsci wrote down his thoughts in the *Prison Notebooks* (1929–1935).

Next to Lenin's photo is Giuseppe Di Vittorio, the first exponent of red unions after the war. In the fifties, he founded Confederazione Generale Italiana del Lavoro (CGIL), or the confederation of workers. Di Vittorio came from southern Italy and was very popular with the man in the street.

Another important picture is actually a map of the Battle of Stalingrad, which was the decisive Soviet victory in 1942 that stopped the German southern advance and turned the tide of World War II. Berlinguer's secretary, Tonino Tato, bought this very original piece in Berlin in the early seventies and had it framed. Again, it was bequeathed to Vezio. "Naturally, I'm very proud to inherit it. This is one of the elements that has contributed to making this small bar of high symbolic value," says Vezio. He has placed photos of Gramsci on one side of the map and photos of Berlinguer on the other.

Vezio's collection includes a number of hanging tapestries, each with its own unique history.

"The Dimitrov tapestry (he was a Bulgarian who was the last secretary of Comintern) is the symbolic center piece of this bar," says Vezio. "This was given to me by Edoardo D'Onofrio, another hero of the Communist Party, and it represents Dimitrov, a distinguished-looking gentleman with moustache and striped tie. On his deathbed, D'Onofrio asked his wife to give this tapestry to me, even though he had children and nephews. It dates from 1950 when D'Onofrio went to Bulgaria."

The handmade tapestry with the head of Lenin has the greatest intrinsic value of anything in Vezio's collection. Pietro Secchia, another party heavy hitter who at one time organized an armed insurrection in Italy, gave this piece to his bodyguard who in turn gave it to Vezio. It originated in one of the eastern republics of the former Soviet Union.

A genuine, battle-scarred, World War II Russian flag from the 14th Soviet Republic, framed because of its poor condition, rounds out the collection.

There is one world inside Vezio's bar, and another outside the door. The bar sits in a building from the 1500s on one of the labyrinthine streets at the edge of the Ghetto, which has been home to the Jewish community in Rome for over 2,000 years.

"Although my family is not Jewish, we have always been on good terms with the Jewish community. I've had many Jewish friends, and my father never sold pork in his butcher shop in order to not contaminate the beef he sold to his Jewish clients," says Vezio.

Following are some highlights of the history of the Jews in Rome. By the thirteenth century, many Jews moved across the river from Trastevere to the Ghetto area. In the mid-1500s, Pope Paul IV said all Jews had to live in the Ghetto and built a wall to enclose a very large number of Jewish people in the incredibly tiny area bordered by Via del Progresso, Via del Portico d'Ottavia, and Lungotevere Cenci. Gates opened at dawn and closed at dusk, and the Pope severely limited the trades they could practice to make a living. Regulations eased up after Pope Paul's death. The French invaded Rome in the early 1800s and Napoleon rescinded the Ghetto laws. In 1848, the ghetto was temporarily abolished, and in 1888, the Ghetto walls were torn down. The year 1904 marked completion of the main synagogue, which sits on the Lungotevere Cenci near Ponte Cestio. During the early part of his government, Mussolini was fairly tolerant of the Jews, but by 1938 his attitude changed and he passed racial laws against them.

The infamous *L'Oro di Roma* (the gold of Rome) incident happened not long afterwards. Two leaders of the Jewish community were summoned to the office of Herbert Kappler, German police commandant of Rome, on Sept. 26, 1943. After initial polite chit-chat, Kappler dropped the bomb: the Jewish community had 36 hours to come up with 50 kilos of gold, otherwise he would deport 200 Jews to Germany.

They scrambled and pulled the ransom together at the eleventh hour—the Catholic Church even offered to make up the difference if they came up short. Kappler's right-hand man, Captain Schultz, weighed the gold on a five-kilo scale in ten increments, and then tried to claim the Jews were five kilos short. In the end, he agreed that there were, in fact, 50 kilos of gold, but refused to issue a receipt. In spite of meeting the German's terms, on October 16, 1,000 Jews were rounded up and deported to concentration camps. At the end of the war only ten returned home.

Today, Jews and Gentiles live harmoniously in the Ghetto area, much as they did a thousand years ago. Every so often, a famous gentile finds his way to Vezio's bar. "One day, myself and some friends were in the back and this guy came in and used the phone," says Vezio. "We weren't paying too much attention. We overheard him call the *portiere* to his apartment building because he had forgotten the code that opens the front door. One of my friends looked up and saw the famous hat… and realized it was the maestro himself, Fellini."

Vezio's bar is near the Campidoglio. The Vittorio Emanuele Monument, Teatro di Marcello, and Trastevere. So whenever you are visiting one of these places or just exploring the picturesque Ghetto quarter of Rome, be sure to drop by. Don't be put off by the out-of-the-way location or low-key entrance. Go inside, talk PCI politics, and order the specialty of the house—te' freddo (iced tea). This homemade drink is a tradition of the Ghetto and Vezio still makes it according to an antique recipe, which is a secret ("Just like the recipe for Coca-Cola," says Vezio). He maintains a high level of quality with cornetti, pastries, and all the products he serves. Plus, as Vezio says, "My prices are not high. I don't want get rich… I want to stay open."

PIAZZA DEL POPOLO

Piazza del Popolo or "the people's square" stands at the apex of a triangle formed by Via del Babuino, Via del Corso, and Via di Ripetta—hence the name for this area, Il Tridente or "the trident." Behind the obelisk in the center of the piazza stands Porto del Popolo, the city's original northern gate. The Trident also has excellent shopping—which is, after all, one of the reasons you came to Rome. Art, antiques, expensive and moderately-priced shoes and clothing, jewelry, watches… it's all here.

Bar Canova

Piazza del Popolo, 16/17
06 3612231
Open 8AM–1AM, Sunday to
Thursday
8AM–2AM Friday and Saturday

Bar Canova was maestro Federico Fellini's unofficial office for twenty years. (He lived just around the corner at 110 Via Margutta.) As Signora Nanda, the owner of Bar Canova, says, "If he left his house in the morning and it was raining and winter, he would go to our backroom and have meetings there. If it was sunny, he would sit at a table outside and watch the piazza… the people. Sometimes the paparazzi waited for him outside, but they never bothered him inside. Times were different then."

"It was easier for him to go to Bar Canova than his real office on the Corso Vittorio Emanuele… He was a lazy man," adds Enrico Todi, friend, former personal secretary to Marcello Mastroianni, Canova regular, and owner of an art gallery on Via Margutta.

"He was at home here," Signora Nanda continues. "He used the telephone by the door. If he wanted some privacy, he'd use the telephone in my office to make a call. My office is very unorganized… disorderly… papers all over the desk. He'd look at it and say, 'How much I like this atmosphere.' And I'd tell him I was ashamed of the mess… and he'd say, 'No this is beautiful… this disorder… I love it.' He was *molto simpatico* (very pleasant).

"The back room was reserved for him and there was a screen across the entrance that allowed him to work in peace. He had a corner that was quiet and tranquil… he met with actors and writers and directors.

"Sometimes he would come here early; have breakfast and then a production car would come to get him and take him to Cinecitta. Other times he would come around 9 or 9:30… according to the appointments he had or what he had to do that day.

"If I didn't see him everyday, I'd think he was sick. We'd say, 'Fellini didn't come today. He must be sick.' Then when he'd come, we'd ask him, 'Where were you for the last three days?' And he'd say, 'I was away…'"

"We were very good friends. For example, at Christmas, he'd come to buy gifts… we make beautiful pastries for Christmas… and he would come running in and say, 'Come here. Advise me what to buy… I don't know what to do. I don't understand these things.' And I'd make a nice basket filled with lentils, tortellini, *zampone* (Modena salami), *panettone*, *spumoni*… good things to eat from Emilia-Romagna… his part of the country.

"He became like family. He was very affectionate with the staff. When he returned from New York, after winning the Oscar for Lifetime Achievement, he came here first... the staff had a party for him... he kissed the pastry cook and the waitress... and joked with everyone. He was a simple person, an exceptional person... very unpretentious. We were so happy for him. He was very content, but this contentment lasted only a little while because he died shortly afterwards."

Fellini, who some call the most visionary and imaginative filmmaker to emerge from postwar Italy, won the Oscar four times for best foreign language film: *La Strada, Le Notti di Cabiria, 8½,* and *Amarcord.* In 1993, he won his fifth Academy Award for a lifetime of service to the industry. Sophia Loren and Marcello Mastroianni were on stage with him, and his wife Giulietta Masina sat in the audience. Not long afterwards, on August 3, the day of his fiftieth wedding anniversary, he suffered a massive stroke and lapsed into a coma. He died on October 31 at the age of 73.

In honor of this talented, yet humble man, Signora Nanda created the Fellini room in the back area of Bar Canova. The walls are filled with Fellini photos and mementos. "After he died... in agreement with his secretary and his wife... we made this room with the things that we got from the people close to Fellini," says the Signora. "I was very upset about his death. I kept expecting him to come through the door. He was the kind of person that you will always miss. His wife died shortly after him...she was also a very simple, unpretentious soul."

In 1950, the year Fellini directed his first feature, Signora Nanda's father commissioned Professore Enrico Del Debbio, renowned Italian architect, to design Bar Canova. During the Fascist period in Italy, Del Debbio created the master plan for a sports and park complex called Foro Mussolini (Mussolini's Forum). In 1928, the first stones were laid for the Academy of Physical Education and the Stadio dei Marmi, a sports stadium with 60 colossal statues of naked male athletes made from Carrera marble, each 12 feet high. Both structures were designed by Del Debbio

himself. The Foro Mussolini was officially opened to the public in 1932, coinciding with the Italian conquest of Ethiopia. After World War II, Il Duce's name was dropped from the marquee and the area is now simply called Foro Italico. The actual plan for the sports complex was fully realized in 1960 for the Rome Olympic games with an Olympic soccer stadium, outdoor and indoor swimming pools, lawn tennis courts, basketball courts, running track, fencing halls, and gymnasium. Del Debbio also designed the nearby Ministero degli Affari Esteri (Ministry of Foreign Affairs), which has a flavor of Mussolini's preffered monolithic style, which symbolized Fascist power and his desire to create a second Roman empire.

Cinecitta, where Fellini made most of his films, was another part of Il Duce's grand plan. He opened the state-of-the-art facility in 1937 as a propaganda factory for the Fascists—making films such as *The Siege of the Alcazar* (1940), a co-production with the Spanish government. The studio's heyday as "Hollywood on the Tiber" was in the 1950s when blockbusters like *Quo Vadis* and *Ben Hur* were shot there. During the 1950s and 1960s, an average of 350 Italian films were produced each year, most of them at Cinecitta.

"After Mussolini's fall, Del Debbio was fired from his teaching post at the University of Rome because he was a Fascist… but later rehired due to his importance as an architect. My father and Del Debbio changed the ground floor of this historic, old palazzo to create the business. Before, there was only a small bar in front, and in back was the laundry for the palazzo. We demolished everything and rebuilt. It took two years," says Signora Nanda.

In order to maintain its unique character, all construction in the historical center of Rome is under the strict supervision of the local government. For example, recently when the palazzo that is home to Bar Canova was being restored, it took fifty different color samples to find the shade that would be homogeneous with the other buildings on Piazza del Popolo.

"Our sign, on the front of the building, has been there since the beginning. Today, you couldn't get permission for it. Rosati, which is also on the Piazza del Popolo, doesn't have a sign because they aren't allowed anymore," adds the Signora.

"Del Debbio designed Bar Canova in a style completely different from his other work. The exterior is modern, while the interior rooms have an eighteenth-century look… very chic and beautiful. When the bar opened, people came from all over Italy to see Del Debbio's work—students of architecture were especially interested in what he had done.

"By 1973, times had changed—people began commuting to work, and they stayed in the city for lunch. In order to accommodate them, we added a restaurant and *tavola calda*… and removed the American bar to make room for the kitchen. We had small, elegant coffee tables, which were not suitable for dining. Unfortunately, those had to go, too. Now, Bar Canova is functional, but it's not the same… it was much more beautiful before. In 1993, we also took a partner, Giorgio Trombetta."

Over its lifetime, Bar Canova has attracted a variety of people, writers like Alberto Moravia and actors such as Vittorio Gassman, Marcello Mastroianni, Philipe Nueret, Anna Magnani, and Catherine Deneuve. During the *Dolce Vita* period, Bar Canova was part of the scene and Anita Eckberg was a regular.

Today, many tourists find their way here; business people and politicians come for lunch, and health professionals from nearby Hospital San Giacomo stop in for coffee.

Whether you're shopping in the Tridente area of Rome, visiting Villa Borghese, or checking out Via Margutta, the Spanish Steps, and Piazza del Popolo, you're not far from Bar Canova. Visit the Fellini room, then try some of the excellent coffee and homemade gelato… Fellini's favorite was a gelato misto: *chocolate and zabaglione.*

GranCaffé La Caffettiera

Via Margutta, 61a
06 3213344
Open 9AM–9:30PM, Monday to Thursday
9AM to Midnight, Friday and Saturday
Closed Sunday

GranCaffé La Caffettiera has managed to create a very unique atmosphere: elegant yet unpretentious, like a very comfortable French salon. The owner, Susy Campaiolo, a very elegant woman in her own right, says, "We provide a place that you want to come back to... a calm and tranquil place to meet with friends and talk."

The cafe, which sits on the corner of Via Margutta and Via di Alibert, is popular with professionals who work in the center of Rome: lawyers, politicians, and show business people, and also tourists looking for a nice place to relax and escape the hustle and bustle of the city.

Signora Campaiolo says, "I believe that first someone has to like the space... the physical location inside... then they will frequent it. I'm trying to create an atmosphere that supports Italian artists and their work with book readings, literary presentations, and an area for paintings, sculptures, and photography. There's lots of variety. Many artists do shows here."

She wants people to actually discover her space, little by little. The café is located on a side street in a building that housed an eighteenth-century theater. A light and

airy foyer with seating draws you forward. From there, the space opens into the main room with a large, elegant skylight that illuminates the interior—during the day it seems like a movie set, back lit with natural light. Original period furniture, large mirrors from the 1800s, and comfortable chairs and tables are arranged to convey a sense of privacy, but not isolation.

The building that houses the café, the old Teatro Alibert, has art and drama in its soul. In 1657, Giacomo d'Alibert, adviser to Louis XIII of France, decided to establish himself firmly in the cultural life of Rome. He purchased land in an area called Orti di Napoli (gardens of Naples) and built an operatic theater, Teatro Tordinova, plus a tennis-like court for a popular game of the day called *pallacorda*. When he tried, however, to expand and build another theater he was nixed by Pope Innocent XII, who more or less ran things. It was Giacomo's son, Antonio, in January of 1717, who finished his father's project and opened the Teatro Alibert, considered the most elegant in Rome. Giacomo sold the theater in 1725 and the new owners called it "Delle Dame," but to the public it was still known as Teatro Alibert. It passed through a number of other owners until February 15, 1863 when it was destroyed by fire. Nine years later, another building was constructed, which housed the Hotel Alibert on the second floor and the Accademia Artistica Internazionale on the ground floor. The Accademia moved in 1955, and there were subsequently other businesses on the ground floor, until April 28, 1999, when the Campaiolo family from

Naples, opened GranCaffé La Caffettiera. *La caffettiera* refers to the stovetop coffeepot for making espresso, still used by many Italians in their homes. The family also has two Napoli locations, opened in 1982 and 1986, and another café in Rome at 30 Piazza di Pietra, which started in 1991.

Via Margutta is an excellent place for this showcase GranCaffé because the area was known as the Orto di Napoli and has always had ties with Naples. Nearby is the Vicolo dell'Orto di Napoli where Charles III, king of Naples, started an Artistic Institute to help young architecture, sculpture, and painting students from Naples. In this area, there was also a large colony of Neopolitans as early as the Baroque period.

One theory has it that the street originally got its name from Margutta, a comic character in the French tales that were performed in the area in the 1400s. Another says that when Rembrandt lived here he used to go to a local barbershop called Margutto and somehow the street was given this name. By the 1800s, Via Margutta was filled with inns, artist's studios, and stores selling a variety of merchandise. Franz Listz, the composer, hung out here, as well as the Italian poet Trilussa and the Irishman James Joyce. In 1917, Picasso in the company of Cocteau, stayed at the Hotel de Russie, and eventually took a studio at 53 Via Margutta. The street was also home to Marcello Mastroianni, and of course, Fellini lived here for years. One of the scenes from *Roman Holiday,* the classic romantic comedy with Gregory Peck and Audrey Hepburn, was filmed here. Today, much as it has always been, quiet *palazzi* with internal gardens and hanging terraces, and boutiques and galleries line the Via Margutta.

Signora Campaiolo has worked in the family business since she was eighteen, and she is almost always in Rome these days. "I like Rome, but Naples is my home. I miss Naples because everywhere in Naples you're near the sea... the sea is so beautiful, especially when the sun goes down. The ocean is this thing that's continually moving...I like it when it's serene, when it's agitated, when it's perfect... especially when I have lots of time. Whenever I return, I see the gulls and breathe in the sea air. It gives me energy... charges me, like a battery.

"Rome is beautiful, but it is completely different from Naples. It's not just that Naples is by the sea, it has different rhythm... it's full of life in a different way. Of course, there is the positive and negative. In Naples, you're around lots of people all the time... sometimes too many... but they are enjoyable and full of life... they have a charm...a way of being cordial... of being friends. They are less interested in appearances and more interested in who you are as a person."

At GranCaffé La Caffettiera, all guests are equally important. The signora wants to create an atmosphere that draws people back because they are comfortable, not because it's a "scene" where celebrities hang out. She does not want actors and actresses to come with their photographers, nor does she encourage paparazzi.

"Everything works together to create a feeling. The way the coffee is served. The way the biscotti are on the plate. Presentation is an important part of eating well," says Signora Campaiolo. The service is very classy, with white table clothes and fine porcelain, and the food is impeccable. From lunch specialties like riso bianco *and* melanzane con pomodoro *to a variety of Neopolitan desserts including BaBa rum cake, GranCaffé La Caffettiera brings the specialties and flavor of Naples to Rome.*

Shop Via Condotti, Via del Babuino, or Via Margutta and then have lunch at GranCaffé. "To treat yourself well is good for the spirit," adds the Signora. This is the place to do just that.

Rosati

Piazza del Popolo, 4/5-a
06 3227378
Open 7:30AM–11:30PM, daily

Rosati was one of the early bars in Rome's *centro storico* (downtown). It opened in 1922 on the Piazza del Popolo, and evolved into a hangout for writers, artists, and Roman aristocrats. After World War II, it also attracted actors and politicians. Today it remains one of Rome's best-known bars on one of Rome's best-known piazzas, where Via del Babuino, Via del Corso, and Via di Ripetta converge.

Rosati's manager, Stefano Alfonsi, a dignified, middle-aged man with a deep, sonorous voice, says, "In general, we have two different types of clients. There are the Italians looking for a tranquil place to relax and talk. We have clients who've been coming here twenty years. Some of them even have this ritual... they come here on the New Year's Day. They figure it's a good way to welcome the year and it's good luck for them."

The second type of client is the tourist. Rosati is featured in many Japanese and German travel guides—the bar is an icon, a "must visit" when in Rome. And Rosati's cappuccino is a must try, distinctive because it's made with specially roasted coffee. The cocktail bar service is also exceptional, offering up to 80 different types of mixed drinks. You might want to try the *Sogni Romani* (Roman dreams) made with orange juice and four kinds of liqueur to form a beverage of red and yellow—the very colors of the Roma soccer team and the city of Rome itself.

People come to Rosati for the high quality of service, and because the atmosphere is like a living room or *salotto* in someone's home, with many comfortable chairs and tables. It maintains its original art nouveau interior. Signor Alfonsi says, "Discretion is the byword here. The tradition has always been for people to be able to have a conversation without being disturbed or disturbing others… this goes for everyone: tourist, Roman, celebrity." The celebrities that come to Rosati act like ordinary people. They usually arrive without their "people"—this is not the "place to be seen," but rather the "place not to be seen."

Vittorio Gassman, the well-known Italian stage and film actor, was a regular up until his death in June of 2000. Gassman spent some time in Hollywood in the fifties and was briefly married to Shelley Winters. He lived a few streets away and was in Rosati almost every day. In fact, he celebrated his last birthday party here, in a special room upstairs with many VIPs in attendance, including the mayor of Rome. Rosati did not allow any press to attend—an example of how it guards the customer's privacy. Nevertheless, two paparazzi were caught climbing on to the second-story balcony in an attempt to shoot photos through the windows. They were asked to leave.

In the sixties and seventies, resident celebrities tended to be more of the left wing intellectual variety: heavy hitters like writers Alberto Moravia and Italo Calvino, both major figures in twentieth-century Italian and world literature. Moravia, who died in

1990, was known for both his stark, unadorned style and his fictional portrayals of social alienation and empty sexuality (not the cheeriest of men), while the Cuban-born Calvino gained his reputation writing imaginative fables. He died in 1985.

Pier Paolo Pasolini was also a regular during this era. Best known outside of Italy for his screenwriting and directing, Pasolini used the juxtaposition of incongruous images to expose the emptiness of modern life. He was murdered by a male prostitute in 1975.

Another film great, Federico Fellini, often arrived early in the morning at Rosati with Luciano De Crescenzo, well known in Italy as a writer, philosopher, and actor. He appeared as Sophia Loren's lover in Lina Wertmuller's *Saturday, Sunday, and Monday*. Both men were early risers, and Fellini looked on De Crescenzo as his salvation—someone to hang out with until 9AM when the rest of the world woke up. They'd meet at 6AM in the Piazza di Spagna and then walk down the Via del Babuino to the Piazza del Popolo. This was Fellini's custom until his death in 1993.

Rosati has a guest book filled with signatures of many guests, including the director Roman Polanski, and Harrison Ford, who visited in December of 1999 when he was in Rome to promote a film. In addition, you'll find Italian director Gillo Pontecorvo's name—he made the acclaimed film *Battle of Algiers* (1966), followed by *Burn / Queimada!* (1969) starring Marlon Brando. Apparently, there was much tension on the set between Brando and Pontecorvo—partly due to the fact that Pontecorvo used many non-professional actors. By the end of filming, feelings had gotten so bad that Brando said he would kill Pontecorvo if he ever saw him again.

Whether you're a celebrity from Hollywood, a tourist from Ohio, or a local from around the corner, the staff at Rosati goes out of their way to make you feel comfortable. A perfect example is this anecdote told by Signor Alfonsi, "Two girls about 18 or 19... typical young Italians... baseball hats on backwards... took two steps inside, looked around and, in Roman dialect, said, 'We can't come in here.' I came up to them and asked, 'Why not?' 'We only want a coffee... we see this place is not for us.' I told them to go and have a coffee... no one will bother you. The expression on their faces was priceless. They felt like fish out of water, but to us they were very welcome."

Here's the ideal itinerary for the Piazza del Popolo: First, visit the new improved statues and fountains, cleaned of all graffiti and completely restored to reveal the true subtleties of color in the stone and marble. A permanent Carabinieri Stazione Mobile stands guard to make sure the graffiti does not return. Next, check out Bernini's Porto del Popolo, the most important entrance in Rome for travelers coming from the north on Via Flaminia. Then, see the two baroque churches—Santa Maria di Montesanto and Santa Maria dei Miracoli. And finally, recharge at Rosati.

· 7 ·

PIAZZA DI SPAGNA

Named for the nearby Spanish embassy, this has been an obligatory tourist stop for hundreds of years. At the turn of the century, the area was an English ghetto. After you've admired Bernini's sinking boat fountain, hang out on the Spanish Steps, and visit the house where Keats died. Then, stroll down Via Margutta or Via Condotti and appreciate what the Italians still do better than anyone else: create seductive, irresistible shop windows.

Babington's Tea Rooms

Piazza di Spagna, 23
06 6786027
Open 9AM–11:30PM in winter
9AM–11:30PM, Mondays in summer
9AM–1AM, Wednesday to Sunday in summer
Closed Tuesdays

Why an English tearoom in Rome? Well, it all started back in the 1700s when the English began to gather in large numbers around the Piazza di Spagna. By the early to mid-1800s, popular guide books of the time described this area as a British colony with English shops, English livery stables, and English reading rooms complete with English gentlemen focused intently on the London *Times*.

Mixed in among the Brits were Canadians, Americans, Scottish, Irish, and Welsh. These people usually fell into two categories: the residents and the visitors (who in a sense became residents because in those days travel was exhausting and hazardous, and once you arrived, you tended to stay for a long time). The first thing to do after unpacking your bags was to locate a good doctor because sanitation and hygiene were not strong points of Roman life in those days. Malaria was also a problem, and the houses were cold and damp in the winter. Fortunately, there were six English doctors in the area by 1850, all graduates of the Royal College of Surgeons in Edinburgh, along with English pharmacies staffed by English assistants to fill prescriptions. The writers, sculptors, painters, doctors, lawyers, nursery-maids, and grooms who inhabited this Anglo-Saxon ghetto even had their own place of worship—All Saints Church of England, built in 1882. They had all the comforts of home except one: an English tearoom.

Enter Miss Anna Maria Babington and Miss Isabel Cargill with venture capital of one hundred pounds and a strong desire to start their own business. The two met in London where Miss Babington moved from Derbyshire to create an independent life for herself, and where Miss Cargill, a transplanted Scot, arrived from her home in New Zealand to visit family and mend a broken heart. (Her father had migrated to New Zealand and founded the city of Dunedin.) Miss Babington knew that her one hundred pounds wouldn't go far in London and asked Isabel Cargill to join her in a business adventure in Rome. This was a huge step: in 1892, proper young women didn't just pull up stakes and go to a foreign country as entrepreneurs.

It's not exactly clear who came up with the idea for a tearoom, but the timing was perfect. In addition to the thriving English community in Rome, 50,000 pilgrims arrived to celebrate the Jubilee of Pope Leo XII, along with the "A" list of Europe who came to celebrate the silver wedding anniversary of the king and queen of Italy.

The two women opened their tearooms at 66 Via Due Macelli on December 5,

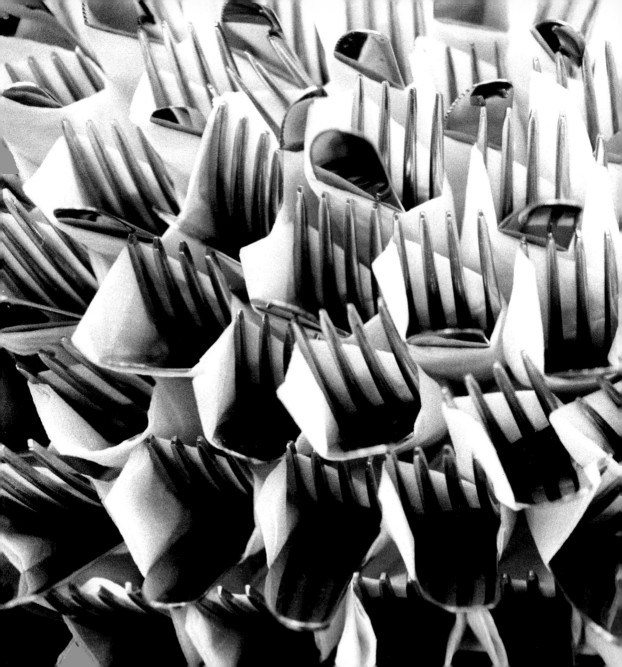

1893, and they were a resounding success. Finally a place in Rome served a "proper cup of tea"—not to mention offering special toilet facilities for women at a time when there wasn't much available, and this was an "unmentionable" problem. Business was so good that they opened a second branch on the Via Rusticucci near Piazza San Pietro (the street was demolished during the construction of the Via della Conciliazione in 1940 by Il Duce and the Vatican).

A few years later in 1896, the two women transferred their business to the current location, with larger premises on the ground floor of what were once stables for a palazzo built in the 1700s. For some mysterious reason, the location near the Vatican was closed.

By 1902, the tearooms had been running successfully for almost ten years. Not only was business good, but Miss Cargill fell in love and married the painter Giuseppe da Pozzo. He was 55 and she was 38. She had been one of the students in his art school called "Academy for Ladies." Da Pozzo was a versatile painter, best known for his portrait painting; his pastel portrait of Miss Babington hangs in the tearooms today.

Two years later their daughter, Dorothy, was born, with Miss Babington as godmother. Babington's continued to prosper (in spite of other tearooms that opened in the area) until the outbreak of World War I when business fell off and Giuseppe da Pozzo suffered a heart attack. In 1919, he died during the Spanish flu epidemic. The 1920s continued to be difficult—Miss Babington was beginning to tire physically and lose interest in the business. Then after the stock market crash of 1929, Miss Babington, whose health had failed, went to Switzerland to recuperate and died suddenly of a heart attack.

Miss Cargill was left to run the business, along with daughter Dorothy, who now had her hands full with four children. To the rescue came Isabel's sister, Annie, from New Zealand, with a little capital and a few fresh ideas. One was to redecorate the interior of the tearooms, which proved to be a resounding success: business picked up immediately. Once again Babington's began to prosper, this time in the thirties during the height of Fascism, which was ironic for a couple of reasons. Italy was becoming increasingly xenophobic and isolationist, and the English tearooms had become a hangout for the "heavy hitters" of the Fascist regime. But while they had tea and scones in one room, around the corner in another, anti-fascist intelligentsia regularly met to discuss Il Duce's misdeeds.

Then in 1939, double tragedy struck: Aunt Annie was killed in a car crash, and soon afterwards World War II was declared. This left Dorothy to care for the tearooms, her aging mother Miss Cargill, and four children. "Her husband, Count Attilio Bedini Jacobini, died in a car accident before the war. He worked for Metro-Goldwyn-Mayer at the time," says Rory Bruce, Miss Cargill's great-grandson, who now runs the business with his cousin Chiara. They reflect the mixed heritage of Babington's. He is blond, handsome, and appears very English, while she has dark, Italian good looks. "My grandmother was left with the money from his insurance policy, which lost most of its value because of the war… so she was basically left with nothing. However with what small sum there was, she decided to build in Cortina and then in Porto Santo Stefano, which turned out to be great real estate investments. Of course she didn't realize this at the time. To her, they were two very beautiful areas. She looked at the natural beauty of things, which put her at the head of the pack. They were small, rural, and charming. When she built there was nothing, and her friends criticized her for going there… 'Why go to a place like this?' they said. She discovered places that are now incredibly popular."

Today Cortina d'Ampezzo in the Dolomites is a premier resort area in Italy, along with charming Porto Santo Stefano. It sits on an island called Monte Argentario just off the Tuscan coast halfway between Rome and Italy, connected to the mainland by a series of three sand spits.

As the war intensified, life in Rome became almost impossible for Dorothy and her family so she moved everyone to her home in Cortina. "My grandmother was stuck up in Northern Italy during the war… Italy was basically cut in half," adds Rory. "My mother was about four or five… there were three brothers, the oldest was eighteen. During this period, the tearooms were run by the waitresses, Giulia, Anita, and Crescenza… they brought in rations… what they got at home… to make a few of the things they used to sell here."

In January of 1944, Isabel Cargill died—the last of the generation that created Babington's was gone. It was unlikely that the tearooms would survive, yet they did. Every morning, without fail, the three loyal employees walked from their homes on the other side of the city to open the business. When food shortages became severe, the resourceful Crescenza improvised with nut croquets, potato-flour bread, chickpea flour scones, and dried chestnut-flour cakes. The women even contributed their own rations of sugar and flour, and only once, on June 4, 1944, did they close for a few hours, when the allies liberated Rome and there was shooting on the street.

Dorothy returned at the end of the war and found, to her delight, business as usual: Crescenza handling the kitchen, Giulia behind the cash desk, and Anita serving the customers. This was the beginning of another phase for Babington's. The

tourists who came after the war were people in a hurry to see as much as possible, the "if-this-is-Tuesday-it-must-be-Belgium" crowd, less inclined to spend time over a quiet "cuppa" and looking for more than tea and cakes. So the next generation of Babington's, Dorothy's children, introduced a menu that included, among other things, aperitifs, wine, and probably the first hamburger in Rome, and they decided to make sure they were serving the best of their signature beverage—tea. This involved many trips to London to sample teas, even carrying a container of water from the Piazza di Spagna to recreate the final product exactly as it would be in Rome. The result was Babington's own blend. Again, the ability to adapt and innovate turned the business around.

"From there it went on to the world-of-cinema phase… from 1960–1975," says Rory. "A period when American and English films were being produced at Cinecitta because it was cheaper. All the actors used to come to Babington's. My mother, uncle, and grandmother were friends with many of them, and my grandmother actually worked for the cinema as a costume designer.

"During this period, my uncle, who had also been a cameraman, started a night club in Rome called the *Strega* (witch). It was an Anglo-Italian sort of thing… he brought English girls from London, who finished school and wanted a year off, to work in his club. This was the first discotheque in Italy, the first place here to have records instead of bands… it was very high class. He had another Strega in Porto Santo Stefano. It got to be quite the scene… Babington's for lunch, the Strega at night… my uncle had the clubs until 1980.

"In the eighties, many Italian politicians used to come here, then we went through a period when the Japanese tourists discovered us. There was even a Babington's franchise in Japan. It started in 1981 and was successful for years, but then the owners went in breach of contract… they began changing recipes and making things they shouldn't have been making. Quality wasn't as good, so we closed it."

Over the years, management of the tearooms has stayed in the family, passing from Miss Babington and Miss Cargill down through Isabel Cargill's line to Dorothy, her daughter, then to her four children and finally to their children, Rory and Chiara, the fourth generation. (Miss Babington had no children.)

The English/Italian heritage is tightly intertwined in Rory Bruce's background. "My mother and her three brothers all had English husbands and wives. My father is English, and my mother is half-English and half-Italian so I'm a bit more English. I lived in Italy until I was six and then went to a boarding school in England for ten years... and then from there I went to Spain where my father was living, and I went to an English school there," explains Rory.

"I grew up speaking both languages, but my Italian was very anglicized... I had an English accent. We always spoke English and Italian at home. But my father left when I was four and the English side wasn't there for long periods of time, so my mother started speaking to me in English. She figured if she didn't I'd lose the English. Of course when I returned it was just the opposite... because my English was much better than my Italian, she spoke to me in Italian. She's bilingual, and so is my cousin Chiara, whose mother is English."

After finishing school in Spain, Rory worked with boats for a while, and then moved to Italy when he was nineteen. "I was fed up with studying when I came to Rome. My mother said, 'Right, you don't want to study, you go to work. Get a job. You have to pay the rent.' This is a very English way of looking at things... in Italy, it normally doesn't happen like this... grown ups spend most of their time at home living on the family until they get married... so I started working in a shop. I worked there two and a half years until I started taking an interest in the family business... that was ten years ago."

Rory's transition from little boy running around the kitchen to actually managing the staff was not exactly smooth. "It was quite difficult in the beginning because there were people working here who remembered me in my crib, and they were much older. We had our massive family lunches in the back room with all the cousins screaming and yelling.... so to come in here and take a different role was not easy. They'd been working here for 30 years and I'd just come in fresh. I had to get into their good books and then start telling them what they should and shouldn't do. I had to learn how everything worked... the kitchen, the waitresses, recipes, and accounting. Slowly I worked my way through the situation. I started off working with my mother... then my cousin Chiara got involved. And my mother started slowly pulling out of the business. She's still the boss, but has left us to run the business. It's very challenging... great fun...we get to deal with lots of people."

Babington's is the place to stop in the Piazza di Spagna area. As you stand in front of the tearooms at the bottom of the Spanish Steps, imagine the area at the turn of century, filled with horses and buggies, and English expatriates overdressed in the hot, Roman summer. Then duck into Babington's for respite and the best cup of tea in Rome, and maybe one of the best in the world. There are twenty-four varieties—Babington's own blend is exceptional. Try a Blushing Bunny (grilled tomato, creamy Italian cheese. and mushroom on toast), Canarino (poached egg on rice pilaf with a tangy cheese sauce), or a Scandian Roll with chicken and mushrooms. Of course, there are always Scottish scones with butter and jam for afternoon tea. Whatever you choose will not disappoint you—and be sure to say hello to Rory and Chiara, always there maintaining the Babington's tradition in a way that would make Miss Babington and Miss Cargill proud.

· 8 ·

TREVI FOUNTAIN

Almost everyone knows this as the fountain where Anita Eckberg and Marcello Mastroianni went for a dip fully dressed in La Dolce Vita. *But before Fellini's film, believe it or not, Trevi was already a must-see for every tourist in Rome. The fact that Nicolo Salvi designed such a large fountain in such a small space is amazing. Plan to view it early or late in the day, when there are no crowds. Afterwards, walk around the neighborhood. Remember in the* centro storico, *you're not far from anything.*

Caffé Accademia

Via del Tritone, 54/55/56
06 6793585
Open 7AM–Midnight, daily

*L*ocated right on the corner of Via del Tritone and Via di Nazareno, Caffé Accademia is a respite from monument or shopping overload. Mariella and Antonio Coteca, the owners, offer the same type of open and impeccable Roman hospitality found at Caffé San Pietro near the Vatican, run by Mariella's brother.

In the summer, when the evenings are hot, it's nice to sit at one of the outside tables on the Via del Nazareno with a cold drink or a *granita di caffé* and watch foot traffic on this main thoroughfare between the Fontana di Trevi and Piazza di Spagna.

As you sit with your back to the café, you face a building that was once a cardinal's home and now contains the Collegio Nazareno, a religious institute attended by primary and high school age students. It was started around 1890 for the children of the nobles. At that time, Italy had a king and there were many nobles at court; this was a very prestigious place for children of the nobility to attend the equivalent of a college preparatory academy.

To your left, and directly in back of Caffé Accademia, you'll see the three arches of an original Roman aqueduct—Acquedotto Vergine. It ran along Via del Tritone

and brought water to the area surrounding the Pantheon. This aqueduct was originally constructed by Marcus Agrippa in 19 AD and restored by Claudius—and it still functions today, supplying water to two of the most beautiful fountains in Rome: the Fontana di Trevi and the Fontana dei Quattro Fiumi in the Piazza Navona. It was restored again by the popes in the 1400s and is the only aqueduct that has been in continual use for almost 2,000 years. Hard to imagine anything we use today functioning in 2,000 years.

There is a legend, represented by a relief sculpture on the Trevi Fountain, that says a young virgin discovered the original spring or source of the water for the aqueduct and showed it to some Roman soldiers—hence the name, Acquedotto Vergine.

Even in ancient times, the demand for water was a problem, and Roman sources, the Tiber, and local springs and pools, were used up as the population of the city increased. The solution was to build aqueducts and import water from outside the metropolitan area.

Of the eleven aqueducts designed as a complete system to distribute water by gravity, only the Acquedotto Vergine was built underground. You see remains of the others scattered around the Roman countryside. These aqueducts supplied a large number of public works: 11 large baths, 856 smaller baths, 15 fountains, 3 lakes or pools, and 1,204 smaller fountains. Rome was the first city in the world to provide water hook ups for private homes. The officials controlled and measured the flow of water to the houses with hand-manipulated gears and animal skin gaskets, and then charged accordingly. You can see the remains of one of these control points in the building directly across from Caffé Accademia on the Via Nazareno.

It goes without saying water is an extremely important element in producing a good espresso. "For example in Naples, they always make good coffee because of the type of water they have. It has much less calcium than Roman water. We use water filters on the coffee machines to sweeten the water, to lower the calcium," says Caffé Accademia's accountant and resident coffee expert who has been with the café since 1958. He is referred to as "Signor Gianni" by Signora Mariella Coteca.

"Here in Rome, and Milan, we have the best blends, but Naples has great water so their coffee is always the best, even if the blend is not. The Neopolitans also put sugar in the coffee because the say sweetness brings out the best flavor," continues Signor Gianni.

"The coffee we use here in Italy is a composition of various types of coffees, mixed like a fine cocktail… according to their characteristics… coffee from Costa Rica, Puerto Rico, Guatemala, Colombia because it's very sweet. The Indian and Zaire coffees have the characteristics that make a good *crema* or head. You want to get the proportions correct for the perfect flavor and aroma.

"The more essential oils, the better the coffee, which gives it the flavor. You roast coffee to release the essential oils. However, it is a fragile food; you have to consume it right away or put it in the fridge, otherwise it becomes acidic. Refrigeration blocks the fermentation of the oils. My advice, if you want good coffee, buy a little from a place that roasts its own… use it right away and then go buy more."

Good coffee is a combination of the water, the mixture and, ultimately, the person that makes it. How much coffee do you use? How firmly do you compress it in the basket? How long do you subject the coffee to water pressure from the machine? A good professional *barista* knows the answers to all of these questions. Even with a semiautomatic machine, the end product still depends on the operator or *barista*.

"Sometimes a coffee made by the *barista* who works the morning shift is better than a coffee made by one who works in the afternoon. The skill of the individual is important. This is especially true with the automatic machines… they produce the equivalent of vending machine espresso: you need the hand of the operator to make a truly good coffee," adds Signor Gianni. "One sure thing to enhance your coffee experience… don't drink it on an empty stomach. The fat and acid will upset your system. It is always better after a meal."

The espresso machine in Caffé Accademia has two nozzles, and, like most of these machines, sometimes the water comes out with more pressure through one nozzle than the other. Adequate pressure is important because if it's too low, you won't get the right *crema* and aroma. A good operator can actually adjust the water so that it comes out of both nozzles with equal force. This skill is the secret behind making a good espresso, time after time—with a perfect *crema* that coats the mouth and is visible all the way down the sides of the cup as you drink.

Caffé Accademia is staffed by people who are all good at their jobs—from the Coteca's two sons, Lucca and Fabio, to Sergio the waiter who has been there 47 years. The day begins at seven and finishes at eleven, with three employees working mornings and three in the evening.

Originally, the business was owned by the Haiti Corporation, a group that imported coffee from Haiti. Next, two brothers operated a typical Roman *salsamentaria* from the location, and then in 1953, a man named Raimondi bought the business and began roasting Colombian and Costa Rican coffee with a wood burning roaster, a slower more natural method than the gas or electric machines used today.

At that time, many places had their own roasting ovens, and the owners piped the fantastic smell of roasted coffee through vents under the doors or windows, drawing people inside. Unfortunately, this custom is now part of the good old days.

There is a myth floating around that says Italians consume more coffee than other Europeans, but this is not true. The average espresso is only 6 to 7 grams, while the Germans and Yugoslavians drink large coffees like Americans: 12, 13, or 14 grams at a time.

Over the years, Signora Mariella Coteca has noticed a change in the attitude of American tourists to the smaller Italian cups of coffee. "When I began working with my brother Franco Rossetti at Caffé San Pietro, Americans came in and asked for a coffee. When they saw Italian coffee in a small cup, they'd hold their hands apart and say, 'big'…'big.' That doesn't happen anymore. The American public is learning to appreciate *caffé Italiano*."

While coffee is popular with some, there are others who are repelled by the bean. "In our house by the sea, we were plagued by ants," says Signora Coteca. "At that time… I'm talking about when I was child… there were no insecticides. My grandmother got some coffee beans and ground them up in this small machine that you cranked by hand. Then she sprinkled this finely ground coffee, almost like

powder, along the ants' trail. They never returned. I think they hated the smell. At the beach, we always ground a little extra coffee for the ants."

This custom of drinking coffee is certainly entrenched in today's world, but it wasn't always like that. Here is a popular version of how coffee was discovered by the West.

In 1683, the Turks laid siege to Vienna. A combination of Austrian, German, and Polish forces overwhelmingly defeated the Turks outside of the city. Their army was routed, and as they fled, they left everything behind: weapons, tents, food, and a large number of sacks filled with strange black beans. A Polish army officer who had lived in Turkey knew exactly what to do with the beans, and claimed them for himself. Soon afterwards, he opened Central Europe's first coffee house in Vienna and eventually became very rich. He also contributed to the evolution of the beverage by filtering out the grounds and adding milk and sugar.

At about the same time, the first Italian coffee house, Caffé Florian, opened in Venice—some say with coffee beans from the same Turkish army. The Venetians, being astute businessmen, began to buy coffee from suppliers and resell it all over Europe. They were the first Europeans to realize that coffee had the potential to be big business.

According to coffee legend, an Arab shepherd in East Africa tending his goats was the first person to discover coffee. Actually the goats were first. During the night, he noticed they acted strangely, jumping and leaping around; even the older ones. Upon investigation, he saw that they had been eating the red berries of a local shrub. He tried the berries himself, and the rest is history.

The speed with which the Romans drink their espresso is legendary in itself—40 to 90 seconds. "We have one client, a very busy and important man on the Italian political scene. He stops here often to have a coffee. The barista sees him come in and immediately fixes his coffee. He drinks with his left hand, so the barista always sets the cup on his left side. The man drinks it in a second. No sugar... very hot... always with his right hand in his pocket. Another half a second... he turns and leaves," says Signora Coteca.

She has two favorite customer stories. The first one involves a classic misunderstanding from the days when an Italian public telephone required a *gettone*—a special coin that you bought from the barista. An American tourist came into Caffè Accademia and asked for a "gin and tonic." Signora Coteca, who was at the cash register, thought he said "gettone," so she gave him a gettone. He took it, went to the bar, and said, "gin and tonic." The barista pointed to the public telephone. The man looked at them like they were both crazy. One more time, "Gin and Tonic." Finally, she understood what he wanted.

The second story is a prime example of the Signora's charm and good will, and political savvy in handling difficult customers. "It was summer and there was an Italian-American woman from New York seated outside who was not happy with her pasta. She didn't like the taste and wasn't going to pay. In protest, she blocked the doorway. She even told people as they walked by that we were thieves. Finally, I told her that what she was doing was not right... that I had showed my good will by offering her something else. She was very tense. I took a seat near her table and we continued to talk... and eventually became friends. In the end she gave me her address in New York and said, 'When you come to New York, visit me.' This was very satisfying.

"Two Spanish women seated nearby saw the whole thing. They told me afterwards that I was very diplomatic. It turns out she had come into the café worried and angry because that morning at the Vatican museum some kids stole her passport and billfold."

Caffé Accademia serves cafeteria-style meals, a cold buffet, ice cream, and bakery goods at reasonable prices—a good place for lunch after visiting the Spanish steps or the Trevi Fountain. For breakfast, there is a selection of cornetti *(Roman croissants) from a recipe by Signor Gianni himself. To make things interesting, little bits of chocolate are hidden in some of the* cornetti. *Find the chocolate and the* cornetti *is free.*

A coffee specialty of the house is crema di caffé: *a spoonful of very concentrated coffee and sugar, whipped until it becomes a cream. This can be added to the café's already excellent coffee as a sweetener and flavor enhancer.*

*Signora Coteca also recommends trying a little flavoring in an espresso—*crema di latte *or* nocciola *(hazelnut), or a* caffé corretto, *espresso with a dash of liquore such as Sambucca, to warm up in the winter. Keep in mind that whatever you order at Caffé Accademia, you can't go wrong.*

Casa della Panna

Via delle Muratte, 85
06 6781435
Open 6am–12pm, Monday–Saturday,
10am–8pm, Sunday (March–October)
Closed Sunday (November–February)

According to one folk tradition, when you toss a coin in the Trevi Fountain, you'll come back to Rome; another says you only have to drink from the fountain to return. Since Trevi water was declared *non potabile* in 1961, even a small sip could significantly decrease your odds of ever seeing the eternal city again. So these days, a coin is your best bet. Some even say the toss has to be over the left shoulder for the desired effect. The tradition existed long before the film *Three Coins in the Fountain* (1954), but it was this story of three women who wish for love by tossing coins in the Trevi Fountain that popularized the idea. The theme song from the film, recorded by The Four Aces, won an Oscar in 1954. You may remember the lyrics:

> *Three coins in the fountain...*
> *Each one seeking happiness...*
> *Thrown by three hopeful lovers...*
> *Which one will the fountain bless?*
> —*Words by Sammy Cahn, Music by Jule Styne*

Fontana di Trevi also had a cameo in *Roman Holiday* (1954) when Gregory Peck tries to con a schoolgirl tourist out of her camera as she stands by the famous landmark. And of course there is the famous scene from *La Dolce Vita* (1960) where Marcello Mastroianni and Anita

Eckberg climb into the fountain fully dressed. She in fact fortified herself with strong drink before she braved Trevi's freezing water for il maestro Fellini.

In case you're wondering what happens to all those coins, according to Silverio Fioravanti, a chemist and son of the former owners of Casa della Panna (House of Cream) located almost next door to the famous fountain, once a week the city checks the chlorine level, cleans the *vascone* (basin), and collects coins and gives them to the Italian Red Cross. Dottore Fioravanti's family took over Casa della Panna in 1930 and recently sold the business to Stefano Pace, who was specially selected as a buyer because he agreed to maintain the identity of this small family business.

Casa della Panna started as a *latteria* (small dairy) in 1915, a time when there were perhaps fifteen or twenty *latterie* in Rome. The *palazzo* (building) that houses the bar/gelateria was constructed around the turn of the century from an old Roman wall. In the basement of the structure, Signor Serafini, the original owner, ran what was in essence a dairy farm in the middle of the city. You can still see his sign on the side of the building: *servizio a domicilio, latte per bambini, vaccheria (dairy farm), caffè latte, crema, burro.* He milked his cows and sold milk products directly to the people who lived in the area until new sanitary hygienic regulations were adopted, and it was illegal to keep cows in an urban setting. From then on Signor Serafini's milk came from the central dairy in large *bidoni d'alluminio* (aluminum cans). It was treated much like wine by the clientele. They came with a bottle or container and got a liter, half liter, or quarter liter of milk served with a standard measuring device. Eventually, the entire process was "closed"—a *latteria* could sell only sealed containers of milk.

"My uncle Settimio Moroni was the first proprietor in our family. My father, Solimando Fioravanti, took over in 1929 or 30," says Dottore Fioravanti. "He expanded and began selling cream, whipped cream, and dairy products. The business became known for its fresh whipped cream, and from this came the name Casa della Panna. It was essentially a *latteria* and a *gelateria* in this period. The bar and *buffet freddo* (cold buffet) came in the 1960s. The interior was redecorated a few times... originally, it had mosaics with a classic, marble *bancone* (counter) and white or gray chairs and tables. The stables became a storage room or small warehouse.

"In the old days, people came to us to get cakes specially made with cream, in particular, *zuppa inglese* (cake with brandy and whipped cream), and they traveled a long way, sometimes a day and a half, from Sicily, from northern Italy and even outside of the country. They came all this way because of the high quality of the products.

"Also, in those days, people would stop by for half an hour or an hour but now it's three to five minutes... you see the pace of life speeding up before your very eyes. Everything is faster and more detached."

Stefano Pace, who took over Casa della Panna in March of 2000, began his career working in a bar/gelateria as assistant to a master gelato maker. From there he attended a *scuola alberghiera* (hotel school) in his hometown, Bari, in the province of Puglia. As Stefano says, "When I was a boy, I lived near a restaurant. In the afternoon, I'd go there and they'd give me a little food and I'd help the waiters, and

I fell in love with the place. I didn't like to study but I decided to go to a hotel school to deepen my knowledge of the industry… I went to school for three years… and studied many things, including French, English, mathematics, biology, and chemistry. There are many hotel schools in Italy… some are very professional and the course lasts up to five years. With others, the course is only six months, and you don't learn much.

"After that, I lived in Glasgow, Scotland for three years, where I met my wife, Elizabeth Carberry. We worked in the same restaurant… it was like a bolt of lightning. She was beautiful… I was captivated by her. She was a finalist in the Miss Scotland contest… if she were a little taller she would have won. She had offers to do modeling, but in the end she chose love…I was a lot more *bello* (handsome) in those days. Anyway, we lived together for four years. Then we got married in 1981… in Italy, everyone says when an Italian marries a foreigner, after a month they leave each other, but we've been together for 20 years. And we have two nice sons… Christian and Daniele.

"At home we speak Italian. This was my wife's choice, because in the beginning, when the boys were babies, she spoke only English to them. When they went to their grandmother or aunts and asked for something in English no one could understand them… so they cried. My wife decided to speak in Italian. They understand everything in English, but speaking it is another matter, because they don't get much of a chance to practice. This year my oldest son, Christian, went to a school in Boston on an exchange program for a month. In the morning he went to Harvard to do some courses, and in the afternoon he was free. The family he stayed with said that after two days he was speaking really well. The same family sent their son to Italy and he stayed with us. It was a very positive experience. Our youngest, Daniele, went to Scotland to visit his relatives... and little by little he got better... in fact he called me on the telephone and was speaking in English. It was very satisfying."

When Stefano Pace returned to Rome, he began working as a waiter at Il Ristorante al Moro, a famous restaurant on a *stradina* (small street) near Casa della Panna, and stayed there for twenty years. As he describes it, "I was responsible for one of the dining rooms. It was a job that I liked very much." During this time he got to know Signora Silvestri Fabiola, Dottore Fioravanti's mother, and when she decided to sell the business she offered it to Stefano even though she had three other buyers. She knew he would continue the tradition of Casa della Panna in a time when more and more small businesses are selling to a *societá* (corporation).

"My wife was a little worried in the beginning," says Stefano, "because for 20 years I worked for a salary, which was a more relaxed way of life. I had to convince her that this was the right thing. I said, 'If we want to change our future this is what we should do. Working for others can be satisfying, but if you have a new idea or a good idea, the boss has to like it. Here, I am the boss.' And also it's good for the kid's self-image... when someone asks what their father does, they say he owns the Casa della Panna near Fontana di Trevi."

Everyone is active in the "family adventure" as Stefano calls it. In addition to two employees, his wife waits on tables, and his oldest son helps on weekends by working the bar. The *specialitá della casa* (specialty of the house) is *granita di caffé con panna*— to create it, Stefano chops ice by hand, mixes it with coffee, lets it solidify, and then adds whipped cream. But this is no ordinary whipped cream—it's made according to a top-secret recipe that came with the business. "It's the only thing I will never change," says Stefano. "I've changed the entrance and I want to replace the floor inside and tables out in front. I've made other small modifications, such as staying open later to appeal to a younger crowd... many of the existing clientele were elderly. But whatever we do, we'll keep the character of an old business... a small local business."

At Casa della Panna, gelato is made the traditional way, and at this point Stefano's oldest is understudying him as gelato maker, although as Stefano says, "He may choose not to continue in the business. He has other interests... he's studying science and he's an excellent swimmer. Still he helps me when I make gelato and he asks me questions on his own... this makes me feel good."

Regulars who stop in for the delights offered by Casa della Panna, include public servants working in the many government ministries in the area. A significant percentage of the clientele is also made up of tourists in transit to Fontana di Trevi. There's been a fountain at this location off and on since ancient times, but Trevi, as we know it, was restored by Nicholas V in 1485 and subsequently worked on by Bernini and Pietro di Cortona. The death of Pope Urban VIII brought work to a halt until 1732 when Pope Clement II commissioned Nicola Salvi to make Trevi the largest fountain in Rome. He finished 30 years later in 1762, and even today, it is a dramatic experience as you round a corner to see this huge sculpture, renovated to former splendor, bulging into the tiny Piazza di Trevi. For centuries, it was a source of water for both the locals and the Catholic Church, which hauled barrels of Trevi water to the Vatican every week. Acquedotto Vergine, in continual use for 2,000 years, feeds the fountain with the best-tasting and softest water in a city with extremely hard water (high percentages of calcium, magnesium, and salt).

Stefano Pace believes in treating tourists well, because, he says, "It's the right thing to do, and they talk with other people. They tell their friends, if you go to Rome don't go to that bar or this restaurant... or they say, when you go to Rome and you are near the Fontana di Trevi go to Casa della Panna… there is a guy who speaks English and they treat you in *un modo simpatico* (nice way). There are many businesses in Rome that don't bother to treat the tourist right. This is not wise.

"There is a journalist from New York named Daniel Halpern who wrote a book called *Halpern's Guide to the Essential Restaurants of Italy: From Milan to Rome with Notes on the Food and Wine* (written with Jeanne Wilmot Carter). He was in Ristorante al Moro with a colleague and I treated them very well. So in his book he said when you go to Ristorante al Moro, ask for Stefano, you'll be in good hands. Americans did come and ask for me…it was a nice thing. Sometimes they weren't even interested in the owner, they'd say, 'We want to meet Ste…*fano*, where is Ste…*fano*…' I was also mentioned in a Japanese publication… they liked me because I accepted them and their culture."

"One time when I worked at Ristorante al Moro I found a very valuable ring. I knew who it belonged to, but she had gone and I didn't know where to find her. So I saved it… after three or four months, this woman came back to eat. As soon as I saw her, I gave her a little package and said, 'I have a something for you.' She asked, 'What is it?'… and I answered, 'A gift.' She opened it, saw the ring and said, 'Oh my god… I thought this was lost for good. It's very valuable.' She wanted to give me a reward, but I didn't take it—my reward was seeing how she looked when she got her ring back."

After you admire the magnificent Fontana di Trevi (the water is now recycled by electric pumps), visit Casa della Panna and set your cholesterol worries aside for a few hours. Anything with cream is good, especially the caffè con panna *and* granita di caffè. *You can also have nice lunch with the* tramezzini, *salad,* pomodoro e mozzarella, *and more. Stefano's handmade gelato is also excellent. If you want, make a contribution to Stefano and Daniele's (the youngest son) phone card collection. They have a total of 5,000—3,000 Italian and 2,000 foreign cards, including Japanese, American, Turkish, and Bulgarian.*

· 9 ·

VIA VENETO & MONTI AND ESQUILINO

Synonymous with La Dolce Vita, Via Veneto was the place to find "the scene" in the mid and late 1950s. Today, the area has lots of banks, insurance companies, big expensive hotels… and the American Embassy. Walk along Via Sardegna, Via Sicilia, and Via Boncompagni running off Via Veneto to see the upper middle class apartment blocks built in the late 1800s, when the Prince Boncompagni Ludovisi, who owned much of the area, took advantage of the real estate boom and sold off his estate. Monti and Esquilino, on the same side of the city, were also developed around the same time, after the unification of Italy. Over the centuries, this quarter was a high rent district for rich Romans, then farmland and ruins.

Lotti

Via Sardegna, 19/21
06 4821902
Open 7AM–10:30PM, Sunday to Friday
Closed Saturday

A drunken Peter O'Toole brawled with paparazzi. Egypt's deposed King Farouk overturned a café table in rage. English actor Anthony Steel lurched at photographers with clenched fists while a buxom Anita Eckberg sat in a waiting car. This was *La Dolce Vita* in full swing, and Luigina Lotti, who was a teenager growing up in a quiet neighborhood just around the corner from Via Veneto, had no idea it was happening. "I lived a very sheltered life," says Luigina, a very sweet and intense woman. "My father would not let the newspaper into the house, and there was no TV. We were prohibited from participating in worldly life."

Italy began to prosper by the late 1950s and early '60s, and the film industry in particular was booming. Rome became the leading center for films shot on location in Europe. A sizeable movie colony sprang up in "Hollywood on the Tiber" which meant the city became an outpost of international café society complete with playboys, socialites, artists, hangers on, and actors on their way up... and down. These last two groups included Kirk Douglas, Deborah Kerr, Ava Gardner, Clint

Eastwood, Lex Barker (an ex-Tarzan), and, believe it or not, Laurel and Hardy. The comedy team made their last film in Europe, a disastrous French-English-Italian production called *Atoll K* (1951), and apparently passed through Rome on one of the live European tours that continued until Oliver Hardy's death from a stroke in 1957.

Celebrity worship in Italy was on the rise—the mobility, leisure, conspicuous consumption, and seeming freedom of foreign film stars made their lives the focus of dreams. After the release of *La Dolce Vita*, while pretenders continued to imitate the film on Via Veneto.

In 1917, when Luigina Lotti's grandparents started the business as a *latteria* (small diary), Via Veneto was little more than a dirt road that ran down from the vineyards and cow pastures that later became Villa Borghese Park. Milk came from the countryside nearby and arrived in front of the store in large cisterns. People then filled up their own bottles. It wasn't until 1946 that the *latteria centrale* or central dairy was formed.

"In those days we sold a mixture of things... milk, cream, biscotti, flowers, fresh eggs, sugar... we even sold breakfast. We have an old license, and we could still sell all of that stuff, including pizza, but we don't have enough space," says Luigina.

"During the war years it was a difficult life. Food was scarce. There was no coffee. Ingredients for gelato were hard to get. Afterwards things started to get easier. When the first American soldiers came to Rome during the liberation, they ate scrambled eggs right in this room. They stayed at Hotel Flora nearby because it was one of the better ones around. This is also where the SS set up its headquarters." Workers from the nearby American embassy still come to Lotti for scrambled eggs.

"My father married when he was older… at 39," continues Luigina, who was born in 1946, "and in our building there were five families in every apartment, a family to each room, with a common kitchen… 100 square meters in total. There were no elevators in the building. We used to hang a basket out of the window to bring up the shopping, so we didn't have to run up and down five fights of stairs. People didn't own their own apartments… one person owned the entire building. We're talking 1940 through 1945 or 1950."

In 1949 Luigina's father expanded Lotti to include a *pasticceria* (bakery), and turned the courtyard into an enclosed atrium or inner dining room. The business was now a bar/gelateria/pasticceria. And, in addition to spumoni and *tortagelato* (a kind of ice cream cake), he specialized in *mimosa* or apple cake, and he even dropped handbills out of a helicopter to advertise his products to the world.

Lotti developed a loyal clientele that included the director of the Istituto Germanico, an archeological school down the street. After the war, when there was a serious plan to rebuild the institute across town, the director said, "There is no Lotti on the Via Aurelia. So we are going to stay here."

The business continued to do well, then in the mid-sixties, misfortune struck. "When I was eighteen, I finished high school, and enrolled in university. At that point, my father had a serious heart attack. Over the years he had worked long hours and demanded a lot from himself. It caught up with him. Now, little by little the business passed over to us," explains Luigina. "Before, I was never here. Girls didn't work in business. They went to school, came home, and studied. So at first I was lost, but slowly but surely, I picked things up. And thanks to the loyal employees who had been with the business for a long time, I eventually got used to things… and I came to really love it.

"I remember very clearly the day he died… May 18, 1972. A few days before his death we rented a house in Ostia to take the kids to the beach. They had to get a polio vaccination so I went back to Rome to have this done. I wanted to get back to Ostia as soon as I could, but he said, 'No, stay another day because we're making gnocchi and it's a lot of work. Stay and help us.' I said, 'Okay, papa… Saturday we're closed—I'll go back then.'

"Anyway, I went back to the house around three or four after I finished working lunch. I heard a noise… a thud. I thought my baby slid out of bed… he wasn't even a year old. But it was my father. I gave him mouth-to-mouth resuscitation… we called the doctor on the floor below… it was too late. And that's how my father died. My mother and I were both present. It was destiny that I came back from the beach so I could be there. Afterwards I had this great desire to make my life successful and dedicate it to him."

In this business you have to have a passion or love for what you do, or it is not worth it. He said to me, 'See the world but keep your feet on the ground and remember you are the daughter of a *lattaio*.'

"This schedule is very rigid and there is really no time to go away on long vacations. You always have to be here for the customers... even though I don't cook or make the pastries... I have many qualified people working for me... but you have to be here. I have one very experienced pastry chef who was fifteen when he started working at the counter for my father. He more or less grew up in Lotti."

Even though this is an old business that appeals to classic tastes, it also has products for the younger market, such as a very unique carrot and orange flavor gelato and animal cookies made with forms that Luigina collects. Many of them come from Germany and Switzerland and they're used to stamp out the shapes of various little animals from Lotti's light, thin dough. The *bambini* adore them.

Then there is the *pasta la rosa* from an old family recipe—layered homemade lasagna-style pasta, with artichoke hearts and a special salami. Originally it was called *pasta carciofi* (artichoke pasta), but Luigina thought *pasta la rosa* was more romantic. This dish is part of the Lotti *tavola calda*, which contains other mouth-watering homemade dishes such as gnocchi and lasagna.

Clients who enjoy Lotti's gelato, pastry, coffee, and *tavola calda* run the gamut from small children to older couples who return and show Luigina the table where they became engaged over afternoon tea. "You haven't changed the place much," they say. "It's almost as we remember."

Office workers are regulars, and particularly those from the American embassy. "This morning the embassy ordered a cake shaped like a Formula Uno for a VIP who loves Ferraris. If I hadn't seen the preparation the day before, I wouldn't be able to describe the cake to them. There are three of us involved in the creation: me, the client, and the pastry chef… and we have to communicate," explains Luigina Lotti.

In addition to being a businesswoman, Luigina is also a bit of a philosopher. "I like to read," she says, "and if you read a lot you can't help but think." To her ice cream is a type of communication, as is pastry: "I think preparing a meal or any food with care communicates that care or love."

About *La Dolce Vita* days she says, "Life during the war was hidden, everything was repressed, secretive, kept in the family… it had to be this way for survival. When the war finished, a sense of well being or prosperity returned, along with more freedom. Before, you could think certain things but not do them. Afterwards, thought became action."

The closest thing she got to rubbing elbows with the celebrities from those days was twenty years ago when she used to take her young son to Villa Borghese Park and run into Anita Eckberg with her baby boy.

If you're going up Via Veneto, walk quickly by Café de Paris where Brando hung out when he was young, and continue past Café Doney—Tyrone Power, Anita Eckberg, Ava Gardner, and Marcello Mastroianni were regulars in the late 1950s. Turn right at Via Sardegna, and at 19/21 you'll find Lotti, the genuine Roman article as it has been since 1917. Excellent gelato, fine coffee, tasty pastry, or a nice lunch. You get it all at Lotti. And be sure to pick up one of their offbeat business cards, painted by Luigina Lotti's talented husband.

Ornelli

Via Merulana, 224
Via Poliziano, 2
06 4872788
Open 7AM–11:30PM, Monday to Saturday
Closed Sunday

Gelateria Ornelli sits on the corner of Via Merulana and Via Poliziano, which explains the two addresses—sort of. Remember, it's Italy. In the days of the Caesars, this beautiful area called Esquilino was a large cemetery. It was built up later on when the government transferred from Turin to Rome after the unification of Italy in 1870, and the eternal city experienced growing pains. The bar/gelateria has been here since 1910; at one time, it was the only establishment of its kind in the quarter. In its early days as a *latteria* or small dairy, it produced its own butter, cream, and milk, and the owners kept their cows in an interior courtyard.

Via Merulana runs straight, past Ornelli, through the Esquilino between San Giovanni in Laterano and Santa Maria Maggiore, which are respectively, the second and third most important churches for Catholic pilgrims. (St. Peter's is, of course, numero uno.)

Adalberto Ornelli, the owner of Bar/Gelateria Ornelli, was born on Via Cavour near Santa Maria Maggiore. He is a charming, friendly man who obviously likes people as much as gelato.

"I come from a family of restaurateurs," he explains. "We had a restaurant about fifty meters from here. When I was a boy, I would 'escape' from the restaurant and come here to get a gelato. I loved the old gelato machine they had. In those days, there were five classic flavors: *nocciola*, *cioccolato*, *limone*, *crema*, and *fragole*."

Signor Ornelli earned a diploma as an electrical technician, but decided he liked to eat and drink too much so he stayed in the restaurant business. In 1967, he married his wife, Anna, and they worked in the family restaurant, Trattoria da Ugo, until 1970 when he bought the gelateria next door. The family juggled two businesses for a while, and, in 1972, the older Ornelli sold the trattoria.

"I tried to improve things. We remodeled, and widened the scope of the business, concentrating on gelato as it was 'once upon a time,' made with fresh milk, cream, eggs, sugar, and fresh fruit. We have 28 flavors, which we change seasonally depending on when the fruit is available. Right now peaches are in, so we make peach gelato. Soon the melons will be ripe and we'll do *gelato al melone*. One of my big successes is raspberry gelato," says Signor Ornelli.

"We have other flavors all year around…classic ones like *gelato di crema*, made with 6 eggs and 200 grams of cream for every liter of milk. We also make a nice *cassata Siciliana*, with ricotta, Sicilian pistachios, candied fruit, milk, and cream.

"My wife works here with me, and we've raised four sons while running the business. At the moment, one of my sons, Alberto, helps us. I hope he'll carry on the tradition. I've been here for 30 years and from day one, never felt like I was in prison or in a cage. I work twelve to fifteen hours a day, but it is doing something that I love."

Adalberto Ornelli's wife, Anna, an open and attractive woman, attests to his love for his work. "*Mi mette le corna con il gelato*," she says. "I tell him that his lover is the gelateria.

He loves his work so much that sometimes he spends more time inside the business making gelato, than outside with his family and wife. For example, he wakes up and starts immediately planning projects for work, and I say today is a holiday, and he says, 'So what.' I help keep him balanced. I think we're a well-matched couple."

The Ornellis have two favorite stories that are testimonials to the high quality of their product. One day Anna Ornelli saw a woman and her three-year-old daughter, occasional customers, walk by heading toward a neighboring gelateria. As they got to the doorway of the rival establishment, the little girl said, "No, no. I want to go to Ornelli." This is a scene Signora Ornelli sees often, "Three, four, and five-year-olds… when their parents give them a chance to choose between our gelateria and the one nearby, they always choose ours," she says. The little ones know.

So do the older ones—appreciation of Ornelli gelato has no age boundaries. A young woman who lives 300 meters from Ornelli works as a caregiver for a 95-year-old woman. Part of her daily ritual is bringing gelato to the woman. Sometimes when she is in a hurry to get to her job, she grabs something from the gelateria below her apartment, instead of

Ornelli. When this happens, the old woman always says, "Today, you didn't go to Ornelli." The young woman told Signora Ornelli, "I must be stupid to think that a woman of her age wouldn't know the difference."

Pellegrini (pilgrims) pass by here en route from the basilica of San Giovanni in Laterano to Santa Maria Maggiore. Tourists also find their way from the Colosseum. Join them, and try the incredible gelato or Signor Ornelli's latest creation: frozen yogurt, made especially for the American tourists.

Buy a cone or a cup and then walk around the neighborhood like the Romani. Palazzo Brancaccio is just down the block. Actually, it takes up an entire block. Built between 1880–1885 by Prince Salvatore Brancaccio, a member of a patrician family, and his wife Mary Elisabeth Field, the daughter of a wealthy New York banker, its halls were decorated by a famous painter of the period named Francesco Gay. The story goes that the palazzo was constructed with her money, and then eventually taken over by the state because the couple didn't pay their taxes. Some things never change.

CAFÉ LISTINGS

Bar Trilussa p. 15
Viale Trastevere, 76
06 5809131
Open 6:30AM–9PM, daily

Caffé Accademia p. 152
Via del Tritone, 54/56
06 6793585
Open 7AM–Midnight, daily

Caffé Sant' Eustachio p. 41
Piazza Sant'Eustachio, 82
06 6816309
Open 8:30AM–1AM, Thurs. to Tues.
Closed Wednesday

Caffé San Pietro p. 80
Via della Conciliazione, 40/42
06 6864927
Open 7:30AM–7:30PM, daily

Casa della Panna p. 162
Via delle Muratte, 85
06 6781435
Open 6AM–Midnight, Mon. to Sat.
Closed 10am–8pm, Sun. (Mar–Oct.)
   Sun. (Nov.–Feb.)

Gelateria Pellacchia p. 86
Via Cola di Rienzo, 105
06 3210807, 06 3210446
Open 6AM–2:30AM, Tues. to Sun.
Closed Monday

Giolitti p. 34
Via Ufficio del Vicario, 40
06 6991243
Open 7AM–12:30AM, Mon. to Fri.
7AM–2AM, Saturday
Closed Sunday

GranCaffé La Caffettiera p. 127
Via Margutta, 61a
06 3213344
Open 9AM–9:30PM, Mon. to Thurs.
9AM to Midnight, Fri. and Sat.
Closed Sunday

Lotti p. 172
Via Sardegna, 19/21
06 4821902
Open 7AM–10:30PM, Sun. to Fri.
Closed Saturday

Ornelli p. 181
Via Merulana, 224
Via Poliziano, 2
06 4872788
Open 7AM–11:30PM, Mon. to Sat.
Closed Sunday

Pasticceria Bella Napoli p. 68
Corso Vittorio Emanuele, 246
06 6877048
Open 7:30AM–9PM, Sun. to Fri.
Closed Saturday

Rosati p. 132
Piazza del Popolo, 4/5-a
06 3227378
Open 7:30AM–11:30PM, daily

Tazza d'Oro p. 48
La Casa del Caffé
Via degli Orfani, 84
06 6792768
Open 7AM–8PM, Mon. to Sat.
Closed Sunday

Vezio's or Bla Bla Bar p. 108
Via dei Delfini, 23
06 6786036
Open 7AM–8:30PM, Mon. to Sat.
Closed Sunday